AN OASIS OF FAN PALMS IN A MOUNTAIN ARROYO.

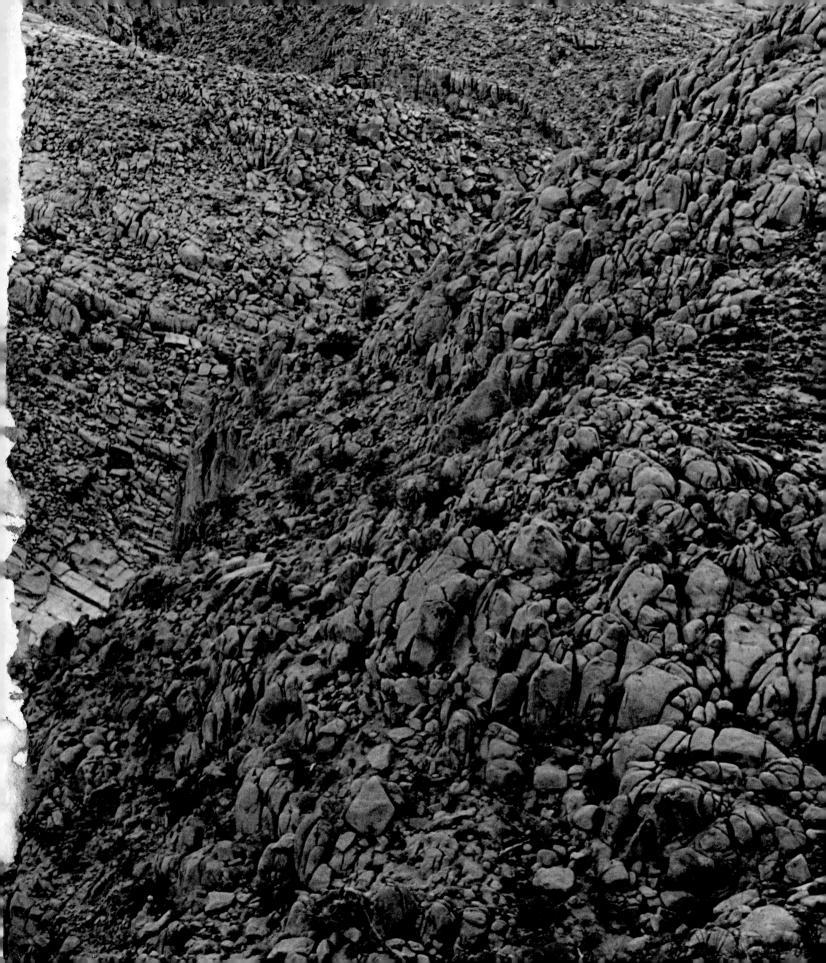

THE GULF OF CALIFORNIA UNDER A RISING SUN

A FOREST OF GIANT CARDON CACTI GILDED BY EVENING LIGHT

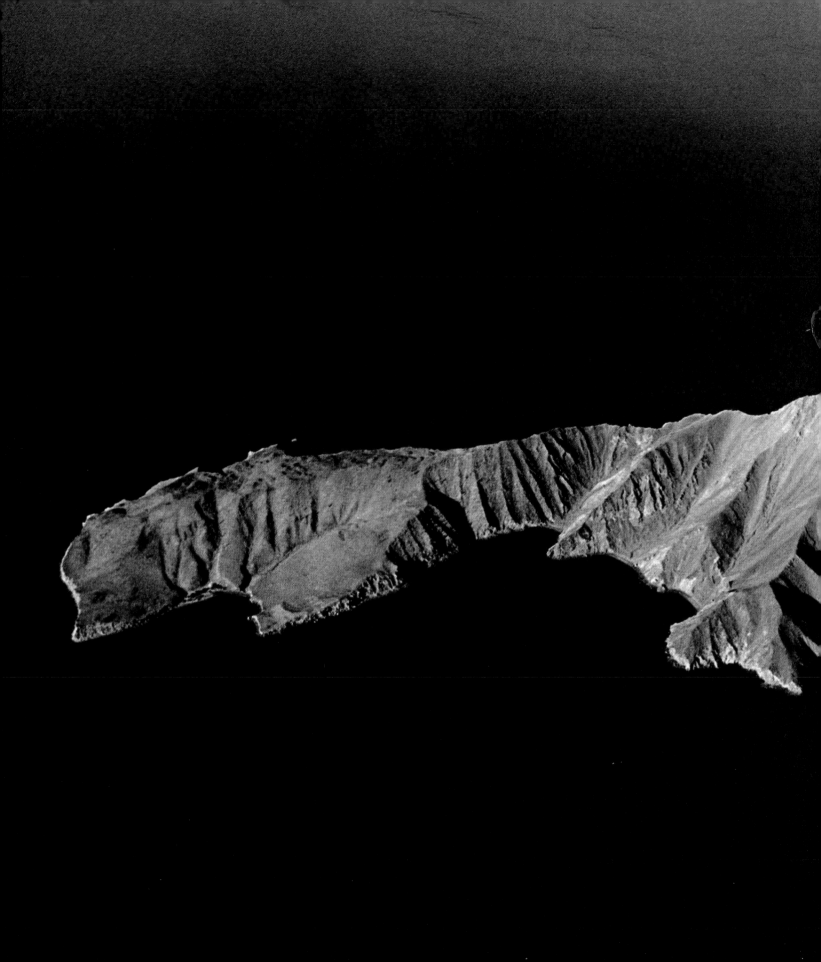

MIRAMAR ISLAND, FORMERLY DEAD MAN'S ISLAND, IN THE GULF

A BACKWATER OF SCAMMON'S LAGOON FRAMED BY A SAND CLIFF

CIRIO TREES IN THE HILLS NEAR SAUZALITO

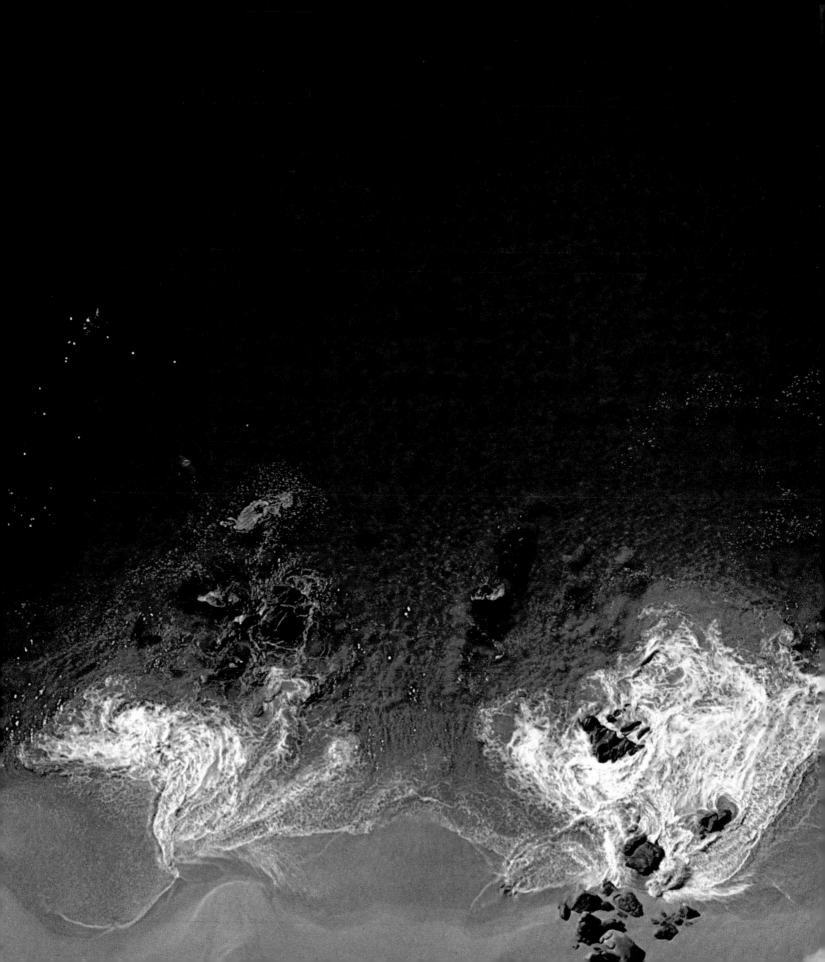

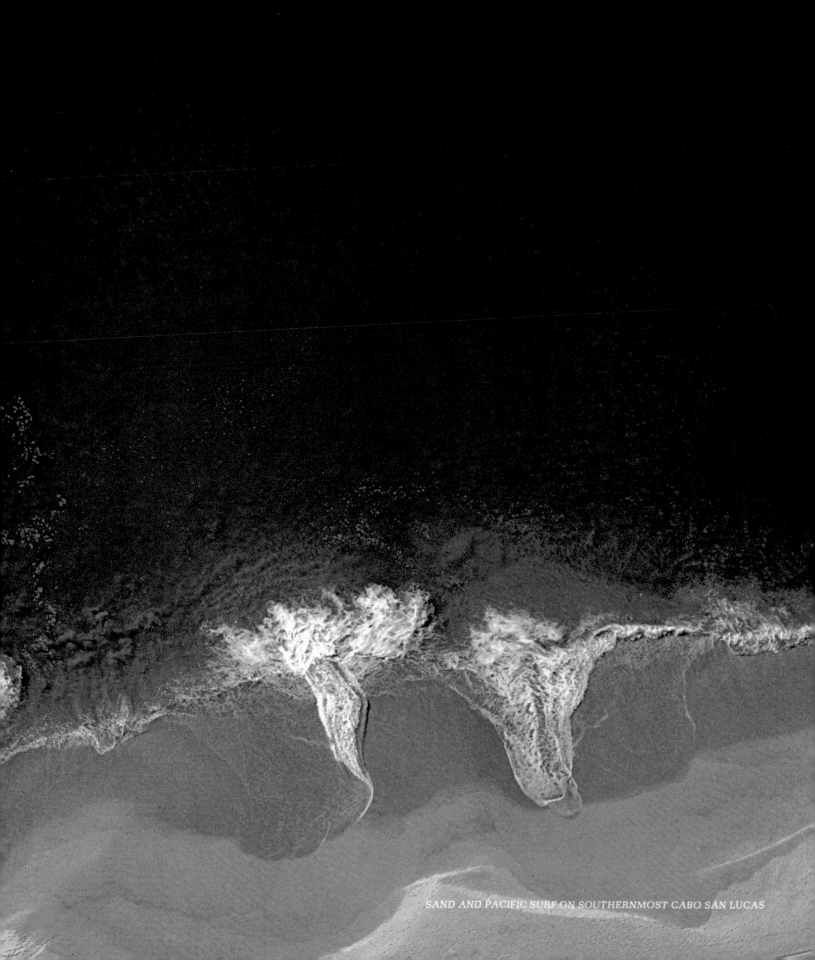

SAND AND PACIFIC SURF ON SOUTHERNMOST CABO SAN LUCAS

BAJA CALIFORNIA

THE AMERICAN WILDERNESS/TIME-LIFE BOOKS/NEW YORK

BY WILLIAM WEBER JOHNSON
AND THE EDITORS OF TIME-LIFE BOOKS

WITH PHOTOGRAPHS BY JAY MAISEL

THE AMERICAN WILDERNESS

SERIES EDITOR: Charles Osborne
Editorial Staff for *Baja California:*
Text Editors: Jay Brennan, Harvey B. Loomis,
David S. Thomson
Picture Editor: Mary Y. Steinbauer
Designer: Charles Mikolaycak
Staff Writer: Gerald Simons
Chief Researcher: Martha T. Goolrick
Researchers: Doris Coffin, Angela Dews,
Margo Dryden, Villette Harris,
Helen M. Hinkle, Ruth Silva
Design Assistant: Mervyn Clay

Editorial Production
Production Editor: Douglas B. Graham
Quality Director: Robert L. Young
Assistant: James J. Cox
Copy Staff: Rosalind Stubenberg,
Eleanore W. Karsten, Barbara Quarmby,
Florence Keith
Picture Department: Dolores A. Littles,
Joan Lynch

Valuable assistance was given by the following
departments and individuals of Time Inc.:
Editorial Production, Norman Airey, Nicholas
Costino Jr.; Library, Peter Draz; Picture
Collection, Doris O'Neil; Photographic
Laboratory, George Karas; TIME-LIFE News
Service, Murray J. Gart; Correspondent Edward
Deverill, San Diego.

The Author: William Weber Johnson lives at Warner Springs, California, in desert-mountain country not far from the border of Baja California. He has been a frequent traveler in that lonely peninsula. He was a war correspondent during World War II and later TIME-LIFE bureau chief in Mexico and Argentina. He is the author of two books in the LIFE World Library: *Mexico* and *The Andean Republics.* He also wrote *Heroic Mexico,* a history of the Mexican Revolution that won the Commonwealth Club gold medal. He is professor emeritus of journalism at the University of California at Los Angeles.

The Consultant: George E. Lindsay, director of the California Academy of Sciences, has been interested in Baja California since he traveled its length as a college student. He has returned often to Baja as leader of research expeditions for Stanford University, the San Diego Natural History Museum and the California Academy of Sciences. He is the author of more than 30 scientific papers and reports on the peninsula.

The Photographer: Jay Maisel, a native of New York City, was educated at Cooper Union and Yale University, where his studies of painting and color had a formative influence on his photographic art. His work has been featured in many magazines and he has had seven one-man exhibitions; photographs he took on a trip through Iran will soon appear in book form.

The Cover: Silhouetted at sunset, giant cardon cacti guard a stretch of the Pacific coastline near the southern tip of Baja California. The cardon is the largest of 110 species of cactus that flourish in the deserts of the peninsula.

Contents

High and Dry, Long and Rocky

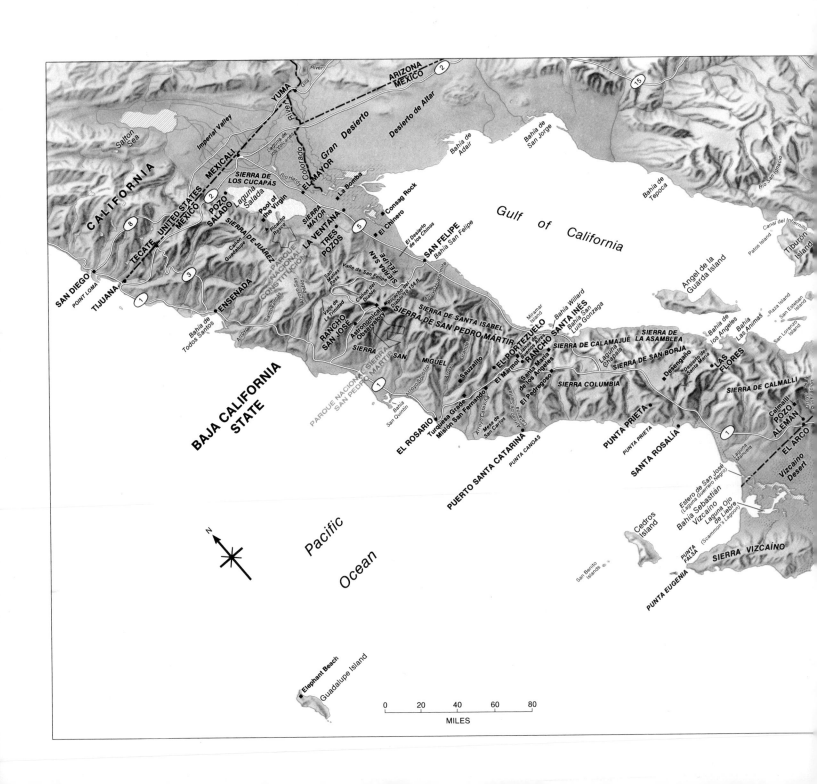

ARIZONA
MEXICO

YUMA

CALIFORNIA

Salton
Sea

Imperial Valley

Laguna
de los Volcanes

Gila River

Colorado River

MEXICALI

Gran Desierto

Desierto

Desierto de Altar

Bahía de
Adair

Bahía de
San Jorge

UNITED STATES
MEXICO

TECATE

POZO
SALADO

SIERRA DE
LOS CUCAPÁS

Río Hardy

EL MAYOR

La Bomba

Laguna
Salada

Pool of
the Virgin

SIERRA
MAYOR

Consag Rock

Bahía de
Tepoca

Río San Ignacio

Gulf   of   California

SAN DIEGO

Point Loma

TIJUANA

SIERRA DE JUAREZ

Picacho
Risco

LA VENTANA

TRES
POZOS

El Chinero

El Desierto
de los Chinos

SAN FELIPE
Bahía San Felipe

Canal del Infiernillo

Tiburón
Island

Cañón de
Guadalupe

PARQUE
NACIONAL
SIERRA
CONSTITUCIÓN

Patos Island

Angel de la
Guarda Island

ENSENADA

Bahía de
Todos Santos

Arroyo Santo Tomás

San
Matías
Pass

Valle de San Felipe

SIERRA

SAN

FELIPE

Picacho del
Diablo 10,154 ft.

Arroyo Matomí

Miramar
Island

Bahía Willard

SIERRA DE SANTA ISABEL

Bahía San
Luis Gonzaga

Bahía de
Las Animas

Raza Island

San Esteban
Island

RANCHO
SAN JOSE

Valle de
La Trinidad

Cañon de
Diablo

Astronomical
Observatory

SIERRA DE SAN PEDRO MÁRTIR

EL PORTEZUELO

RANCHO
SANTA INÉS

SIERRA DE
LA ASAMBLEA

San Lorenzo
Island

SIERRA

SAN

MIGUEL

Arroyo Grande

Sauzalito

El Marmol
Llanos de
Santa María

SIERRA DE CALAMAJUÉ

Laguna
Chapala

Bahía de
los Angeles

Desierto de
Santa María

LAS
FLORES

PARQUE NACIONAL SIERRA
SAN PEDRO MÁRTIR

San
Bahía
San Quintín

Arroyo Socorro

Santa María
de los Angeles

El Pedregoso

SIERRA DE SAN BORJA

Desengaño

SIERRA DE CALMALLI

BAJA CALIFORNIA
STATE

EL ROSARIO

Turquesa Grade
Misión San Fernando

SIERRA COLUMBIA

Calmallí
POZO
ALEMÁN

Mesa de
San Carlos

Arroyo Catavinía

PUNTA PRIETA

Punta Prieta

SANTA ROSALÍA

EL ARCO

PUERTO SANTA CATARINA

Punta Canoas

Punta Canoas

Laguna
Manuela

Vizcaíno
Desert

Estero de San José
(Laguna Guerrero Negro)

Bahía
Vizcaíno

Bahía Sebastián
Vizcaíno

Laguna Ojo
de Liebre
(Scammon's Lagoon)

Pacific
Ocean

N

Cedros
Island

San Benito
Islands

PUNTA
FALSA

SIERRA   VIZCAÍNO

PUNTA EUGENIA

Elephant Beach
Guadalupe Island

0   20   40   60   80

MILES

Baja California is a geographic anomaly in almost every way. Its 55,000 square miles are only about one third of the total area of American California, but the peninsula is 800 miles long. As shown in the detailed relief map below, Baja is very largely a land of mountains and uplands—the highest points are marked by black triangles—but much of the peninsula is desert, which by definition receives less than 10 inches of rainfall a year.

Streams (blue lines) often run dry (broken lines), and its biggest dry lake, Laguna Salada (blue stippling), is a good deal more imposing than any of its ordinary lakes or swampy lowlands (blue stripes). Baja has numerous towns (black dots) but only five main roads (double black lines with circled route numbers); it also has two national parks (red outlines and red type). Points of special interest are designated by black squares.

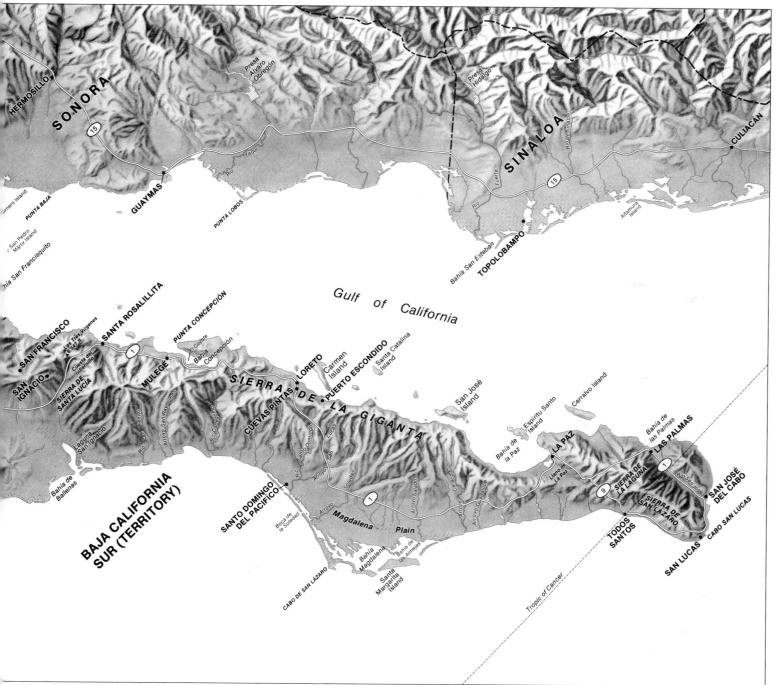

HERMOSILLO
SONORA
15
Presa Alvaro Obregón
Presa Hidalgo
SINALOA
CULIACÁN
Río de Sinaloa
Turners Island
PUNTA BAJA
San Pedro Mártir Island
Bahía San Francisquito
GUAYMAS
Río Yaqui
PUNTA LOBOS
Río Fuerte
Río
Bahía San Esteban
Altamura Island
TOPOLOBAMPO
15

Gulf of California

SAN FRANCISCO
SANTA ROSALILLITA
PUNTA CONCEPCIÓN
Las Tres Vírgenes 6,547 ft.
Cuesta del Infiernillo
SAN IGNACIO
SIERRA DE SANTA LUCÍA
El Coyote
Bahía Concepción
1
MULEGÉ
LORETO
CUEVAS PINTAS
PUERTO ESCONDIDO
Carmen Island
Santa Catalina Island
SIERRA DE LA GIGANTA
San José Island
Espíritu Santo Island
Cerralvo Island
Bahía de las Palmas
LAS PALMAS
Laguna San Ignacio
Arroyo San Raymundo
Río Santo Domingo
Río San
Arroyo Soledad
Arroyo Calafia
LA PAZ
Bahía de la Paz
Llano de La Paz
1
SIERRA DE LA LAGUNA
SAN JOSÉ DEL CABO
Bahía de Ballenas
BAJA CALIFORNIA SUR (TERRITORY)
SANTO DOMINGO DEL PACÍFICO
Boca de la Soledad
Magdalena Plain
Bahía Magdalena
Santa Margarita Island
Bahía de las Ánimas
9
SIERRA DE SAN LÁZARO
TODOS SANTOS
SAN LUCAS
CABO SAN LUCAS
CABO DE SAN LÁZARO
Tropic of Cancer

1/ The Indomitable Peninsula

Here is no water but only rock
Rock and no water and the sandy road
The road winding above among the mountains.

T. S. ELIOT/ *THE WASTE LAND*

The most consistently unclouded, clearly visible detail of North America seen from an orbiting space vehicle is a slender and misshapen finger of land dangling from the southwestern corner of the continental mass—a peninsula extending some 800 miles from the United States border to well below the Tropic of Cancer. Panoramic photographs taken by astronauts invariably reveal this peninsula, called Baja (Lower) California, with startling clarity. The rest of the continent may be obscured by cloud cover, haze or the blankets of smoke that hide the great cities. But Baja California, in pictures taken from 110 miles up, is almost always sharply and minutely recorded—a region of tumbled mountains, yawning chasms, desert plains, lonely shores, barren islands. It appears to be wholly unmarked by man, untouched by man's busyness. The checkerboard patterns of cities and towns and the grids of fenced and cultivated land are lacking. So are the string-straight lines and calculated curves of highways. So are the mirror surfaces of rivers, lakes and ponds, for this is an almost totally arid land. Hence the great clarity of the air and the vast emptiness. At the first distant glance, the peninsula appears to be without life—tawny, bare, wrinkled, all sand and rocks.

That Baja California should be so plainly seen from afar presents a certain irony. Except for a few towns at the extremities, north and south, and a handful of oases in between, comparatively little of the peninsula is seen by the earthbound—and this in an age when not much of the world is left unseen or uncrowded.

Baja California is twice the length of Florida and 100 miles longer than Italy. Like Florida and Italy it is bounded on one side by a gulf, on the other by a sea. More than a thousand miles of lonely Pacific shoreline lie on the west. The eastern boundary, somewhat shorter, is formed by a body of water that has been variously known in the past as the Sea of Cortez, for the Spanish conqueror of Mexico, and the Vermilion Sea; it is now called the Gulf of California.

But this peninsula is not like either Florida or Italy. It is not quite like any other place on earth. The Gulf of California separates it from the rest of the republic of Mexico, of which it is a part but with which it has little in common aside from the intangibles of politics and language. It has far less in common with its neighbor to the north, the United States, from which it is separated only by an arbitrarily drawn, 150-mile-long border that extends from Yuma, Arizona, west to the Pacific Ocean. Above the line lies one of the hemisphere's most densely populated regions, the state of California, called Alta (High) California by the natives of Baja California. Below the line—once you are past the hustling border cities of Tijuana and Mexicali—lie some 55,000 square miles of empty or almost empty wilderness.

Sierras, or mountain ranges, form an almost unbroken spine from the northern border of Baja to the southern tip at Cabo San Lucas, a cape where the peninsula suddenly ends in a tangle of sea-sculpted rocks plunging into the 1,500-fathom depths of the Pacific. The sierras are a continuation of the mountain system that parallels the west coast of the North American continent from the Aleutian Islands south. Here in Baja California the mountains are massed along the eastern coast, where they rise abruptly, in some cases almost vertically, out of the Gulf of California and the desert littoral. The western slopes are more gradual, slanting toward the Pacific, so that the peninsula seems to be tilted toward the setting sun.

The highest mountains are in the north, in the sierras of Juárez, closest to the border, and San Pedro Mártir. The highest point of the peninsula is Picacho del Diablo, or Devil's Peak, a 10,126-foot pile of gray-white granite that thrusts up into the cloudless sky from the San Pedro Mártir. From October to May it is often snow clad, frequently visible both from mainland Mexico, 140 miles away, and from far out in the Pacific Ocean.

To the south of these sierras are lesser ranges—Santa Isabel, Santa

María, Calamajué, Asamblea, San Borja, Calmalli, San Francisco, Santa Lucía, Giganta—barren, forbidding and traversed only by a few hazardous passes. Their flanks are cut with canyons and arroyos carved by forgotten torrents, each ending in a dry alluvial fan on the desert floor. At the southern end of these ranges the peninsula flattens out, narrowing to less than 30 miles just above the territorial capital of La Paz. Then, in the cape region, the mountains rise again in the comparatively verdant and well-forested Sierra de la Laguna.

Most of Baja California is desert and receives less than 10 inches of rainfall a year. Parts of the country may go for four, even five years without a drop of rain. Baja's desert—classified by scientists as part of the great Sonoran desert system that covers much of Arizona, northwestern Mexico and southeastern California—consists of three principal areas. In the northeast, where the Colorado River peters out in the Gulf of California, the river delta becomes a narrow bone-dry plain that extends perhaps one third of the way down the peninsula. On the west coast two desert areas stretch almost unbroken from El Rosario, approximately 200 miles below the United States border, to the cape region. In the southern part of this stretch, called the Magdalena Plain, underground springs have made some farming possible. North of the Magdalena Plain, at mid-point on the west coast and extending inland to the peninsula's mountainous spine, is the area known as the Vizcaíno. This central desert is an awesome wilderness. Some of it is bare sand, some is clay and some is rocky—a moon landscape of gigantic boulders and jumbled fragments. Its western reaches receive some moisture from the fogs and damp winds off the Pacific, but generally rains are rare.

Yet despite the aridity of the central desert, parts of it support one of the most astonishing assortments of desert vegetation in the world. Some of the plants are tiny to the point of invisibility. Some are gigantic grotesques, nightmare things. Some are beautiful, giving the low-keyed landscape a dash of color and a sense of symmetry on a horizon of flat planes and sharp angles. Some form impassable barriers with sharp thorns and barbed spines. Some are poisonous; others are life givers, providers of food and drink in the desert. A great many plants are endemic—found nowhere else on earth. Baja's natural barriers—seas and mountains as well as deserts—have created biological pockets in which strange species, such as the bizarre *cirio* tree and the monumental cardon cactus, have developed and survived by adapting themselves to an adverse environment.

From 100 miles up, a camera in the Gemini 5 spacecraft captures both the earth's curvature and the southern end of Baja. To the right of the peninsula lies the Pacific, to the left the Gulf of California, widened by the Bahía de la Paz. Popcornlike clouds hover low over the tropical region at Baja's tip.

This same ecological isolation affects the animal world of Baja. Behind the natural barriers, in the canyons and mountain valleys, in the lagoons and on the offshore islands, peculiar species have developed: a rattlesnake that has no rattles, a black jack rabbit, a bat that catches and eats fish. The isolation also offers peculiar attractions to migratory creatures. The elegant tern, for example, may fly 5,000 miles or more from the west coast of South America to one small, lonely and otherwise insignificant island in the Gulf of California to scratch a nest in the sand and lay its eggs. The gray whale—the farthest traveling of all mammals—migrates once each year from Alaska's Bering Strait region to the lagoons of Baja California, a round trip of 10,000 miles or so, to breed and to bear its young. Both the elegant tern and the gray whale are species that have in the past been pushed to the brink of extinction by man's depredations—egg hunting and whaling. But in the loneliness of Baja California they have found the freedom and the safety they must have to survive.

Some of the world's wilderness areas remain so because they are inaccessible, like the Gobi Desert or the upper Amazon. Others, such as the Australian outback, have lasted because of a poverty of the material rewards that lure men to remote corners of the earth. Still others, fortunately, are perpetuated as wildernesses because of a thoughtful government. They are set aside for controlled human recreation or for the preservation of endangered species—as is the case with the various national parks and monuments of the United States and the magnificent game preserves of Africa.

The reason Baja remains a wilderness seems to be none of these, but rather a sort of indomitable stubbornness, a built-in resistance to the destructive impact of civilization, to the erosion caused by man's technology and acquisitiveness. Few of the world's wilderness areas have been so dreamed about, so dressed with fantasies, so desperately scratched over by men eager for wealth or power or renown. For more than four centuries man has been attempting to subdue the Baja peninsula, physically or spiritually, to exploit it or at least make it do his bidding. For all this human effort, most of the peninsula clings stubbornly to its primitive state. Much of it remains as it was a thousand, perhaps even a million, years ago.

Everywhere there are signs of this resistance, scraps of men's dreams: ruined missions, adobe walls blasted by the abrasive wind, trails that lead nowhere, bleached bones, abandoned mines, wrecked machinery.

First came the Spanish conquistadors, avidly searching for gold, a passage to the Indies and a mythical race of lady warriors who fought with golden weapons under the rule of a queen named Califia (for whom the Californias were ultimately named). Califia's realm had been celebrated in a popular medieval romance, *Las Sergas de Esplandián (The Exploits of Esplandián)*, dealing with the adventures of a prince who gathers a crusading army from various nations to defend Constantinople against an assault by the King of Persia. The narrative told of a contingent of troops from California, "an island on the right hand of the Indies, very near the terrestrial Paradise, peopled by black women among whom there was not a single man. They had beautiful, robust bodies, spirited courage, great strength. Their weapons were all of gold . . . because in all the island there was no metal except gold." Few of the Spanish conquerors could read, but many of them knew the story and had heard of California. The search for Amazons (and their gold) played an important role in spurring the exploration of the New World, including the discovery of a mighty river in South America that was, naturally, called the Amazon.

After the gold-seeking conquistadors came a succession of priests who tried to convert Baja California into a kingdom for God. Then followed a motley procession of adventurers, buccaneers, pearl divers, speculators, land promoters, surveyors marking boundaries between nothing and naught, revolutionaries, prospectors, miners and, always, treasure hunters. There is something about a barren country that inspires the belief that it contains hidden riches, waiting to be uncovered by the prospector's pick or the modern treasure hunter's electronic detecting device.

Despite the discouraging lessons of the past, there are still a few hardy souls—ranchers, farmers, fishermen, true frontier people—who live in and with the country. They are isolated, hospitable people who gladly share what little they have with friends and strangers alike: the shade of a single tree, a gourd cup of sweet spring water, a bunch of grapes, a chunk of crumbly white homemade cheese, a strip of dried meat. They accept the country on its own hard terms—and in turn they are accepted by it. Their intrusion is minor, their marks on the land few and insignificant.

The traveler who is willing to accept the Baja California wilderness in the same spirit will find it a land of lonely grandeur, mystery and subtle beauty. Strange, yes, monstrously so, and stark and uncompromis-

What seems to be the result of a recent rockslide is actually a pile of granitic boulders formed perhaps 80 million years ago. These giants, which dwarf the six-foot-five-inch-tall man at lower right, began as a blob of molten rock beneath the earth's crust. Before reaching the surface, the granite cooled and shrank and developed incipient fractures. Once the rock was exposed, moisture crept into the cracks, froze and split the mass into what is now a mammoth heap of granite chunks.

ing, too. But its secret places and its ringing silence have a way of lifting the heart and inspiring wonder.

The silence seems to intensify toward the center of the peninsula. One night I camped in a grove of cardon cactus at El Portezuelo, a narrow pass in the hills south of Laguna Chapala, a dry lake. The broad lake bed had been thick with suffocating dust, as dry and desolate as the planet Mars, and it was a relief to get past it. My campsite was at least 30 miles from the Pacific, but with darkness a damp, chill wind came from the ocean. Within a few hours the temperature dropped from searing heat to about 50°, and in the quiet I could hear moisture that had accumulated dripping from the car.

Then, from far away came the sound of a truck, its gears grinding on a grade to the south. The sound continued for a long time, and finally the truck arrived, noisily, at my campsite. It proved to be loaded with empty gasoline tins. The driver was disappointed that I had no cigarettes but welcomed a sandwich. He drove on and for another long stretch of time I could hear the grinding gears and the rattling cans. Then I heard no more and I knew that the truck was down in the sound-deadening dust of the Chapala lake bed.

Again I was in a silent world—until my hearing adjusted to the subtle night sounds. The whirs and clicks of insects. A wood rat stealthily gathering sticks and twigs. A mouse cracking seeds. Later, in the middle of the night, coyotes off somewhere in the distance—the direction is always puzzling—singing in tones of anguish and jubilation. Then, before first light, the liquid notes of the mockingbird and the stuttering of the cactus wrens. Then the nervous clucking of some desert quail as they took cover in a thorny thicket, and the insistent hammering of a Gila woodpecker chiseling a hole in a cardon trunk, a hole that would become a tidy, weatherproof shelter for the woodpecker or for an elf owl that might preempt it.

But as daylight comes the desert world grows silent again. Most desert animals hunt and eat at night, the birds at dusk and dawn. They hide from the heat of the day. So animal movement ceases except for a buzzard soaring high overhead, hovering, barely moving. You become aware of your own breathing, the scuff of your boots in the gravel, the snapping of twigs as you walk. You begin to feel that you and the light are the only things that move and change. The morning sky has gone from deep purple rose to orange to glaucous yellow and finally to a cerulean blue in which the sickle moon fades and disappears. The giant cacti, which had seemed menacing and vaguely ambulatory in the starlit darkness, now start to assume their proper proportions. They are still huge, still grotesque, but they become lifeless, timeless, as motionless as stones. Their shadows shrink, and when the sun is overhead all shade is gone and there is killing heat, a blinding, sterile waste. To rid your mouth and throat of the feeling of gritty cotton you sip water judiciously from your jug, bearing in mind the way some Baja Indians taught their children to drink—only while holding their breath and only taking as much as one held breath would permit. Burros and mules have similar good sense about water in the desert. Horses and human visitors have to be restrained from drinking themselves sick or, worse, exhausting the supply.

The hours pass and the shadows grow again, leaning toward the east. In this country of blazing sun and clear air the shadows have an impenetrable darkness—so dark they seem to be vacuums in the spectrum. Fog banks and clouds move inland from the Pacific, making the tops of mesas and mountains seem to be floating in the sky. After a final burst of fire the sun drops into the clouds and you are left in a gray void, a world fast becoming cool and dark, gloomy and foreboding. As you move on, searching for another place to camp, you are, as always in Baja, struck by the feeling that this is an ancient world, either dead or nearing death, devoid of promise and cheer, inhabited only by ghosts.

But it is not all that ancient; not at least in the millennial measurements that geologists and paleontologists use. The Baja peninsula began to break away from the mainland of Mexico only some 20 million years ago. Before this great geological shifting took place, the Pacific coast of what is now Baja was not desert at all, but warm, humid and lushly vegetated—about like the present-day coastal areas of Georgia and South Carolina. Plants and trees were abundant—palms, conifers, rhododendrons, figs, grapes. Along the shore ranged a variety of monstrous creatures. One of the most startling was the hadrosaur, or duck-billed dinosaur, gigantic in bulk, with tremendous hind legs and a great thick tail. His 1,000 or so teeth were formed into big grinding plates in his cheeks; with them he could demolish aquatic and terrestrial plants as well as crustaceans, which he gathered with his ducklike bill. His fossilized bones have been found in the tortured, multilayered badlands around the coastal town of El Rosario. The largest ever discovered, excavated by William Morris of Occidental College with the support of the National Geographic Society, is about 50 feet in length, with a computed weight of 23 tons.

The hadrosaur's neighbors included other dinosaurs, among them one giant carnivore as yet unnamed but resembling the tyrannosaur, and a tiny shrewlike creature that was one of the early mammals. The latter had teeth no larger than the head of a pin; scientists have had to sift through tons of earth and gravel to find one of them. South of El Rosario, at Punta Santa Catarina, may be found another curious relict deposited by the ocean: the ammonite. A cephalopod—a relative of the squid, the octopus and the chambered nautilus—the ammonite derives its name from the resemblance of its large curled shell to the ram's horn that was the symbol of the Egyptian god Ammon. Natives refer to ammonites simply as *caracoles,* or snails. Their fossil remains were once abundant. The sedimentary banks of the Arroyo de Santa Catarina, several miles inland from the present shore, were richly studded with fossilized shells from 17 to 20 inches in diameter and eight to 10 inches thick, weighing up to 100 pounds apiece. But over the years professional fossil merchants and rock hounds have depleted the deposits.

Still farther south are other fragmentary clues to the peninsula's past. Near Punta Prieta fossilized remnants have been found of a hyracotherium, a primitive form of horse about the size of a dog. In an arroyo at Pozo Alemán, at approximately the mid-point of the peninsula, Mexican scientists have been excavating a fossilized mammoth. This area, now extremely arid, must once have been green to support this herbivorous beast. Apparently it died in a rockslide in the arroyo, for there are no nearby projectile points or other evidence that it was killed by man. Several hundred miles farther south, however, fossilized bones of bison, camel and horse have been found. Some of the camel and horse bones appear to have been burned, suggesting that someone cooked and ate these animals, and a few of the bison bones were split lengthwise as if a man had tried to get at the marrow.

The curious, thoughtful traveler finds himself continually puzzling over man's presence in Baja. When did he come here? Where did he come from? And, particularly in view of the peninsula's perversity in matters man usually considers essential to survival and progress, why? Did ancient man migrate here when the area was still fertile and well watered and then, as years of drought turned the land into desert, find his retreat cut off? Did he drift into this cul-de-sac by mistake? Or was he driven here by enemies in the north? Could he have come from across the sea? For none of these questions are there any conclusive and satisfying answers.

Colossal human figures with extended arms, depicted on a cave ceiling in Arroyo San Borjitas, may have been the Baja Indians' way of giving thanks for game or praying for more. To reach the painting surface—a problem shown by the size of the cave visitor at right —aborigine artists probably used a crude ladder or a scaffold of palm logs.

There is not much evidence that men lived here in antiquity, but there is some. Arrowheads and worked stone can occasionally be found in almost all parts of the peninsula. The best place I know to pick up projectile points and other shaped stone is in the drifting sand and dust of the southeastern end of Laguna Chapala. Near what was once the lakeshore there are granite cliffs eroded into caves and natural shelters. Between the cliffs and the shoreline there must once have been abundant game—deer, antelope, rabbits, hares, birds. Man-made chips and points of gray-green, black and milky white stone are easily found in the decomposed granite gravel and the powdery dust beyond it. But they prove little more than the obvious fact that the people here knew how to chip and flake stone.

Burial sites are scarce and unrevealing; evidently most of Baja's aborigines cremated their dead. Indian graves in mainland Mexico are frequently rich with evidence, not only of the physical man but also of his way of life, his beliefs, his handicraft and arts and treasures. In Baja they tell almost nothing. Evidently few of the original inhabitants were potters. For containers they relied mostly on baskets, animal skins and nets of fiber or hair. Potsherds, useful as date and culture indicators, are occasionally discovered in the northern part of the peninsula but are rare elsewhere.

There are tremendous piles of shells—clams mostly—along both coasts and casually scattered elsewhere the way modern man scatters beer cans. But they prove only that the Indians ate shellfish and that this food was plentiful and delicious. It still is.

Oral history—the folklore, religious or otherwise, that is handed down from generation to generation—is almost completely lacking. Except for a few small tribal groups in the extreme north, the aborigines have disappeared. When the Jesuit missionaries came to Baja California at the end of the 17th Century the native population, never very numerous or dense, was already down to about 50,000 because of the diseases introduced by the Spanish conquistadors one and a half centuries earlier. By the time the Jesuits left after 70 years, the native population had been reduced to about 10,000. By the early 19th Century the Indians were almost all gone. Today there are people with Indian blood in Baja California, but aside from a handful of Kiliwa, Cucapá and Paipai in the north they are mostly descendants of people who migrated from mainland Mexico, the Yaqui principally.

The missionaries, when they came, found no Indian temples, no monuments, no permanent dwellings and little current evidence of the artistic skills that were characteristic of other American Indians. Questioned, the Indians could speak only of present urgencies or problems, with no hint either of racial pride or tribal lore. There was one hint of past glory, however, in the claim of some of the Indians that their ancestors had come from the north and had been people of giant stature and great accomplishments.

That there had once been a people in Baja who were more advanced culturally is suggested by the cave art that exists from one end of the peninsula to the other, as it does in much of the southwestern United States. The abundance of caves and rock overhangs, the dry climate and the isolation of most sites have ensured that much of the cave art remains in a fair state of preservation. Some of the art takes the form of petroglyphs, usually simple designs chipped or pecked or etched into stone walls and ceilings. There are, as well, paintings done in earth colors—red, black, white, yellow. The more ambitious paintings include figures not only of animals—mountain sheep, deer, antelope, rabbits, fish, birds—but also of humans. The latter are usually sticklike, with arms raised in exhortation or exultation, and some are much larger than life size. The paintings often appear to be the work of many hands, possibly of many generations, with much overpainting.

The cave art sites are generally difficult to get to and it is unlikely that the Indians used them as permanent shelters. The first white men to come to the peninsula found that the Indians displayed a sort of claustrophobia. They did not like to have anything overhead. They might take temporary shelter in caves but they seldom stayed there. Aside from occasional tools and arrowheads, comparatively few artifacts have been found in the caves.

Very often the cave paintings are high on the walls or on the ceiling. This suggests that they were executed with considerable effort and were not simply idle doodling. Since they were so often superimposed on one another, even when plenty of empty wall space was available, it would appear that the act of painting was more important than the painting itself—possibly some sort of religious rite. Since the animal figures frequently bristle with lines that could represent arrows or spears, the ritual may have been concerned with the hunt, either thanksgiving for an abundance of game or a plea for its return after depletion.

Most of the caves that contain art are in the side walls of arroyos or canyons, some of which have a trickle of water in the bottom. The water would have drawn game to these areas; once they were there, the Indians could have driven them into the arroyos or canyons as into traps. Many of the animal figures in the cave paintings are portrayed with open mouths, suggesting that they were panting from having been pursued. In the case of animals that are represented as impaled, the arrows seem to enter from the top; the caves may have served as hunting blinds, the hunters shooting down on the driven game.

What do these paintings tell us about the aboriginal Indians of Baja? Nobody is sure, but some interesting deductions have been made by Clement Meighan, an anthropologist at the University of California at Los Angeles. Dr. Meighan was a member of an elaborate expedition to Baja that was organized by the late Erle Stanley Gardner, the detective story writer. An avid searcher for lost gold mines and other hidden treasures, Gardner was fascinated by the mysteries of Baja. Equipped with everything from pickup trucks to airplanes to helicopters, Gardner and Dr. Meighan, in the early 1960s, visited the remote village of San Francisco, high in the mountains north of San Ignacio. San Francisco is near a chasm variously known as the arroyo of San Pablo or San Nicolás or Salsipuedes (literally, "get out if you can"). The two men scouted nine caves in the vicinity of this arroyo by helicopter and then examined four of them closely. The largest cave, some 500 feet long, contained no fewer than 136 portrayals of men and animals. The human figures were simple and angular, the bodies painted red and black, the arms invariably upraised. There were animal figures of deer, rabbits and bighorn mountain sheep.

Through radiocarbon dating and scrutiny of the paintings and artifacts, Dr. Meighan reached some tentative conclusions. The caves had been used as hunting blinds by a nomadic people from the north. At first these people had found that the arroyo attracted several different sorts of animals, as reflected in the variety of creatures pictured in the paintings. But then the country had grown more arid, food resources had diminished, and game may have been overkilled. Greater and greater effort seems to have gone into the paintings—perhaps as a magical means of bringing back the animals. But if that was their purpose, the paintings did not work. The game did not return. The paintings, Dr. Meighan found by radiocarbon dating, had been done some eight centuries ago. But the people, he believes, did not leave the caves right away; they were only abandoned about two centuries before the Spaniards came to the peninsula.

Gardner, less inhibited by scholarly caution, speculated that "this region may have been the cradle of a very important civilization." He also conjectured that the nomads might have belonged to the same mysterious people from the north who invaded central Mexico in the 13th Century, laying the foundations of what became the Aztec federation. No support for this theory has been forthcoming.

Whether there once was a race of Baja Californians of superior culture may never be known. But there is ample evidence that the Indians who occupied the peninsula when the Spaniards arrived had either retrogressed from superior ancestors or may simply not have progressed far beyond the dawn of mankind. One of the Jesuit missionaries described them as "stupid, awkward, rude, unclean, insolent, ungrateful, mendacious, thievish . . . and naïve and childlike so far as intelligence and actions are concerned. They are an unreflecting people . . . who possess no self-control but follow, like animals in every respect, their natural instincts."

Obedience to natural instincts may have been the only thing that made it possible for Indians to survive at all in this country. While other peoples concerned themselves with clothing and shelter, the early Baja Californians devoted virtually all daylight hours to the search for food. They lived almost completely in the open. Only in the most severe weather would they seek shelter behind a temporary barricade of sticks or stones or in a hastily dug hole in the ground. Both missionaries and the Spanish military tried in vain to get the Indians to live in compounds. They went about naked most of the time, although the men sometimes wore fillets of shells and beads in their hair and the women would occasionally don a brief apron of cords and beads. The men were hunters and trackers. The women were gatherers of fruits, roots and seeds. There was seldom an abundance of anything and they utilized an astonishing variety of desert plants for food. When game was especially scarce the Indians would eat rats, mice, snakes, crickets, grasshoppers, caterpillars, spiders, lice from their own bodies, even the skins of dead animals that the buzzards had left behind. After the white man came they developed a taste for eating leather boots. The only animal that was considered taboo was the badger because both its facial features and its footprints were thought to resemble those of a human too closely.

This simple people had no words for rich, poor, young, old, peace, quarrel, truth, shame, faith, love, hope, virtue, vice or virgin—which made conversion to the abstract ideas of Christianity a difficult matter. Nor was there any word for year, nor any idea of time. Chronology was measured only by the successive fruiting seasons of the pitahaya cactus —the most (and perhaps only) joyful time of the year. There are two kinds of pitahaya, the *agria,* or sour, a multistemmed, sprawling cactus with tart red-skinned, red-fleshed fruit; and the *dulce,* or sweet, pitahaya, an upright organ pipe cactus with either red or greenish-white fruit. The fruit of each type is refreshing and nourishing. When it was ripe, the Indians did nothing but gather and eat the pitahaya until they could eat no more. Then they slept until they could continue eating. Why not?—there was no way to preserve the fresh fruit.

Although the Indians of mainland Mexico were in some cases sophisticated mathematicians and astronomers, those of Baja California could use only their two hands for counting. Higher calculations were not necessary; there just was not that much of anything. They were true wilderness dwellers, shaping their lives within the severe limitations of their particular wilderness, achieving a precarious and delicate balance between resources and needs. The struggle to maintain this balance permitted no luxury, no cultural flowering, no accumulation of wealth. And it did not tolerate interference. The arrival of the white man—and his diseases—interrupted the Baja Indians' marginal way of life in the mildest sort of way. At least it was mild compared with the violent conquest and subjugation of the better-developed Indian cultures of mainland Mexico. But while the mainland Indians survived to become a dominant factor in the life of modern Mexico, the Indians of Baja California perished—virtually obliterated by the time the white man got through with his unsuccessful efforts to make Baja California conform to an alien pattern.

A Gallery of Land Forms

Baja California stunningly refutes the notion that the look of desert country must inevitably be monotonous. The peninsula has its unrelieved stretches of sand and rock, its treeless plains and peaks. But even these bleak places reveal a strange beauty when viewed from fresh vantage points, and together they demonstrate that Baja's land forms are decidedly diverse. The photographs by Jay Maisel on the following pages record the beauty as well as the diversity, a joint triumph of nature's artistry and engineering.

Baja's unique appearance is the product of both its geologic past and its almost moistureless present. Its vividly contrasting features stem in the main from the characteristic way in which each of its kinds of rock has withstood or yielded to the forces of weathering and erosion. Chief among Baja's basic materials is granite—the so-called basement rock that underlies a large part of the peninsula and still dominates the lofty mountains of the north and the rugged uplands of the south. In central Baja the granite is covered by sedimentary rock, much of it laid down when this part of the peninsula was submerged in ancient seas. These sedimentary layers are capped by massive sheets of lava and other volcanic materials later set loose by prodigious movements within the earth's crust beneath Baja.

Each of these kinds of rock can take myriad forms—depending on climatic conditions and erosive forces. Wind is one such force on Baja; a more decisive factor is water. Baja gets so little precipitation that when rain does fall its erosive action on the thin soil and bare rock is disproportionately violent.

This meager moisture has sundered the granite slopes of the north and created mosaics of shattered rock (right). In the central plateau, Baja's most arid area, water's erosive effect is even more spectacular —the result of downpours after years of total drought. These fall on vast expanses of soft sedimentary rock that becomes deeply gullied, intensifying its denuded, jagged look.

The seas that flank Baja also account for some of its most striking features. Constantly on the attack, the Pacific and the Gulf of California flatten, pound, build and shape everything from the delta of the north to the level sands and sentinel rocks of Cabo San Lucas, remodeling Baja's rugged outlines even as other forces transform its interior.

Crisscrossed with cracks, the boulder-strewn granitic highlands of Baja's Sierra de Juárez attest to the mighty power of a little moisture. Water seeps into the deep fractures and shallow cracks, then freezes at night, forming levers of ice that pry open solid rock and enlarge the maze of fissures.

A network of tidal channels (left) in the delta region of northeastern Baja carries sea water inland at high tide from the Gulf of California, adding to the salt flat (top) created by evaporation. The delta plain was formed of silt deposited by the Colorado River before the building of upstream dams reduced its rust-red torrents to a trickle. The delta area includes 2,000 square miles of Baja's gulf coast—plus sections of California, Arizona and the Mexican mainland.

Deep canyons, gouged out by the runoff from rare desert rains, twist downslope from the 1,500-foot-high Mesa de San Carlos. This immense table of stratified rock, 15 miles long and six miles wide,

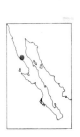

is made up of sedimentary layers topped by a thick lava sheet. The hard lava has resisted erosive downpours, but the softer sedimentary layers, exposed to the elements on the mesa's flanks, have been vigorously scoured and shaped by rushing rain water.

Descending to the sea in steplike ridges, this mountain terrain near *Bahía San Luis Gonzaga* looks formidable enough, but is the only place in the ranges lining Baja's gulf coast where the drop to the water is not dizzyingly steep. The high escarpments along this shore are the result of faulting, which continues to uplift all Baja and tilt it westward.

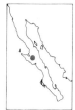

Sand dunes of various types, including crescent-shaped barchans and ridgelike transverse dunes, rear up at the northwestern edge of the Vizcaíno Desert. The sand grains start as bits of rock that become pulverized by coastal currents, which deposit them on beaches to pile up into dunes. Prevailing onshore winds then force the dunes inland.

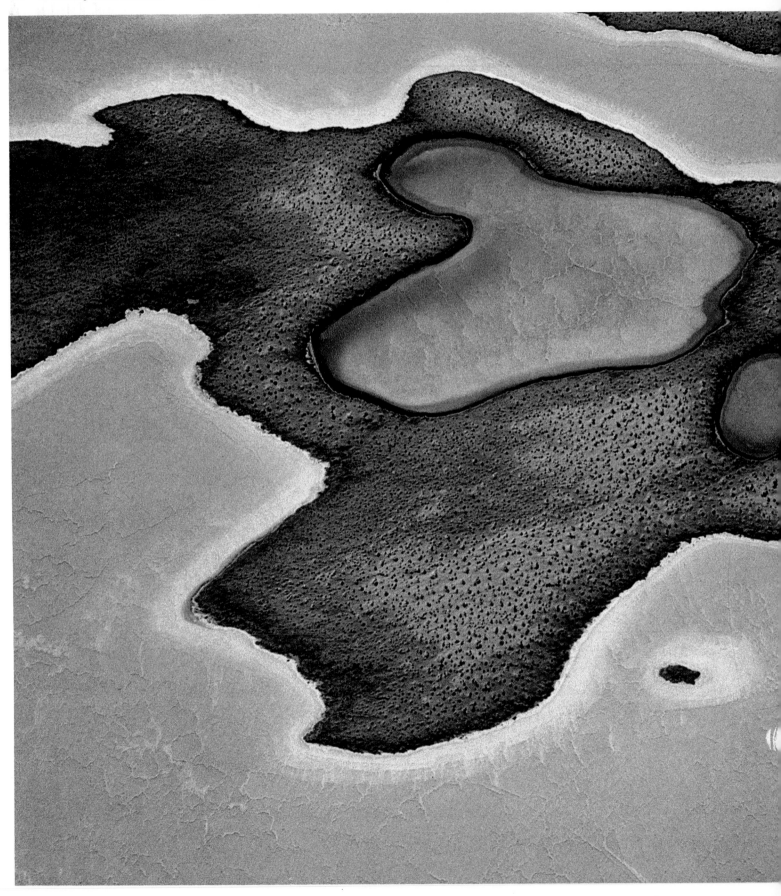

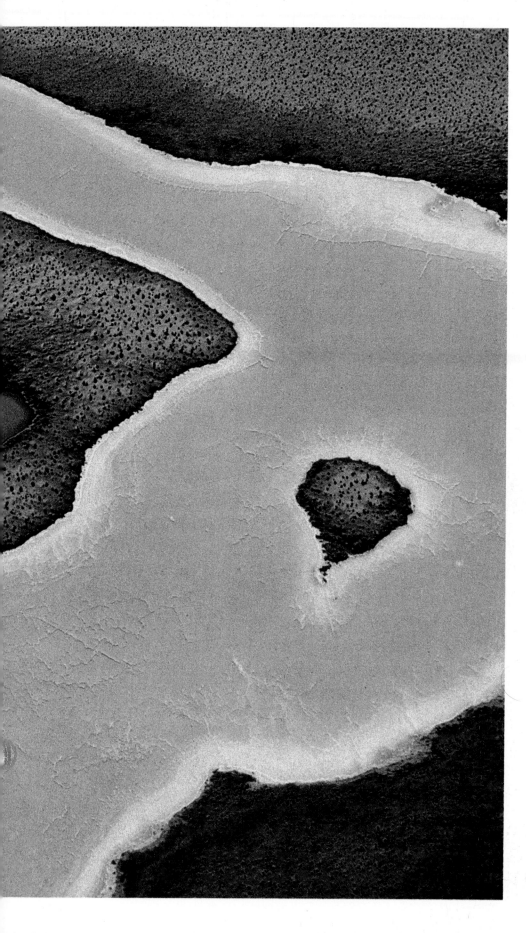

Looking as if some cosmic abstract artist had fashioned them, two small lagoons, one pale brown and one a darker brown, lie trapped by brown-black sand, which in turn is ringed by a larger greenish-white lagoon (shown in part). There are two tiny islands in the large lagoon. These landlocked pools, located near the Pacific coast in the Vizcaíno Desert region of Baja, are periodically replenished by the wind-blown waves of high tides or ocean storms; and as the sea water evaporates it leaves a white crusty residue of salt. The colors of the three lagoons vary according to diverse forms of algae growing in water of differing degrees of salinity.

A tidal estuary near Bahía Magdalena in southern Baja, this sluggish stream winds its way through a dense forest of mangrove trees, then peters out in the desert beyond (top). Mangrove thickets line many of the bays and inlets along this section of the Pacific coast, in some places forming an impenetrable barrier three or four miles wide.

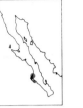

Hewn out of solid rock by violent rains, stream beds of ever-diminishing size branch outward across the Magdalena Plain from a deep main arroyo. Though the channels in this typical desert drainage network were dry when the picture was taken, the moisture they supply sustains hardy plants amid a landscape of naked rock.

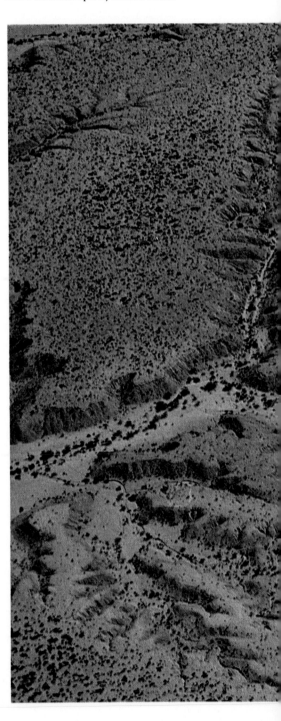

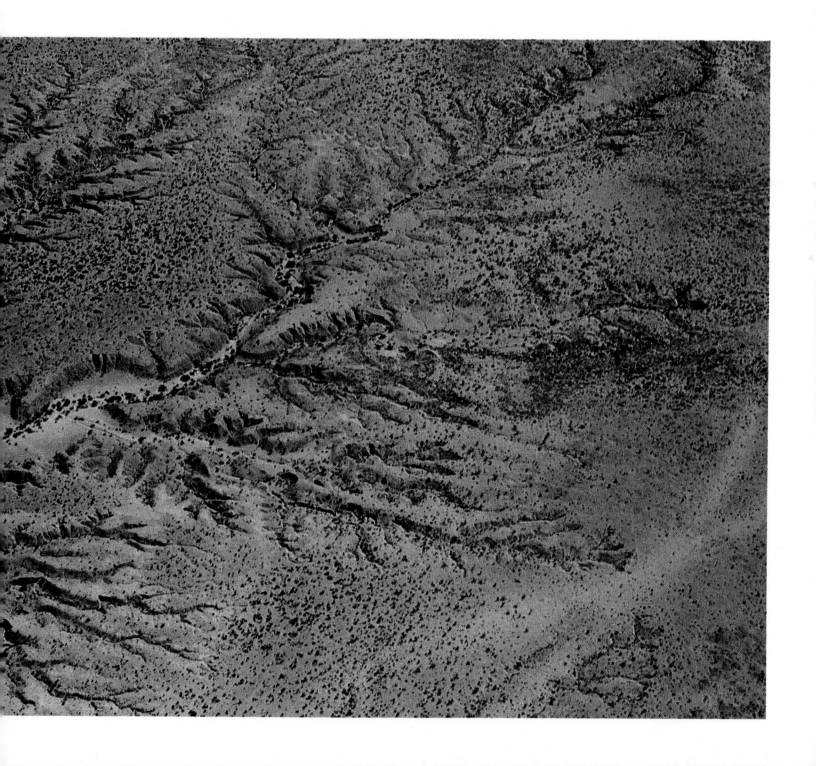

Battered and pitted by countless centuries of erosion, the many-layered uplands of the Sierra Giganta (left) tower above Baja's gulf coast in a weird jumble of jagged cliffs, flat ridges, volcanic peaks, deep arroyos and vast lava sheets. This complex landscape is largely composed of sedimentary rock, some of whose layers were compacted of debris eroded from volcanic formations. The layer of dark greenish rock visible on several cliffs was laid down while the region was covered by the sea.

Espíritu Santo Island rises from the Gulf of California in a series of rock terraces whose great height may be gauged by the 10-foot-tall mangroves edging the shore. While some islands in the gulf are volcanic in origin, most, like Espíritu Santo, are not. Until some 20 million years ago they were part of Baja. As the peninsula split away from the Mexican mainland and moved slowly northwestward, these islands remained as debris in the newly forming gulf.

Giant granite boulders form an imposing rampart beyond a beach at Cabo San Lucas, Baja's southernmost point. Long ago these rocks were part of the peninsula—a solid promontory that jutted  out to sea like a ship's figurehead. But under the steady assault of waves converging from the Pacific and the Gulf of California, the promontory's lines of weakness were probed and enlarged. Eventually, the weaker sections were destroyed, leaving only isolated pinnacles of harder rock.

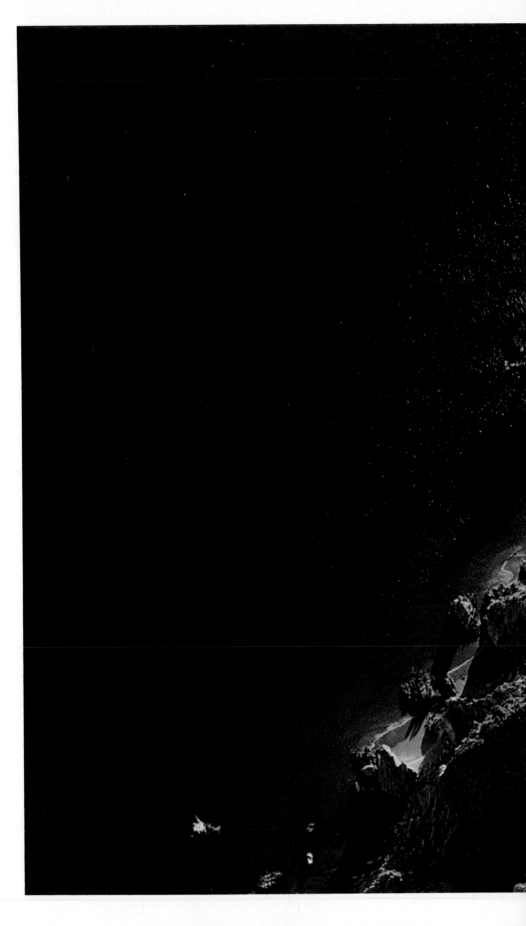

2/ Mud, Sand and Mirages

The very air here is miraculous, and outlines of reality change with the moment.... A dream hangs over the whole region, a brooding kind of hallucination.

JOHN STEINBECK/ *THE LOG FROM THE SEA OF CORTEZ*

To see the Baja Peninsula you can fly to the southern tip and then work your way north, or you can start in the north. The second choice has a certain logic, since you begin near one of the world's most densely populated areas—Southern California—and move into one of the least populated, a country that becomes more empty with every mile.

There are simple ways of making the trip, the easiest by airplane. Chartered planes fly into the smaller settlements, the fishing camps and resorts; almost all of them have an airstrip of some sort. But in this way you miss a great deal in between the airstrips.

If you are truly adventurous you can go by mule down the center of the peninsula along its mountainous backbone. But this method is not recommended. Some years ago a friend of mine, an experienced rancher and hunter who has spent most of his life in the back country of Baja, decided to take a mule train the length of the peninsula along this central route. His starting point was Tecate, a pleasant border town whose principal industries are a brewery and a retreat for overweight ladies. He organized a party of 10 people and a string of 20 mules and set out in December 1963. He planned to reach Cabo San Lucas, the rocky southern tip of Baja, in three and one half months. The route covered about 1,500 miles of ill-defined tracks and trails in mountains, canyons and deserts. This meant making about 15 miles a day.

A mule is sure-footed and can get by on less water and on rougher forage than a horse. At night, unpacked, it will roll in the dirt to ease its back and then set off in search of whatever edible scrub is available. But a mule is not always tractable or predictable. On my friend's venture, a number of mules took off at night and never came back; some, guided by instinct, headed for their home ranches. Among the mules that remained, some weakened and had to be traded for burros at wayside ranches. Some lost their footing in rock-strewn arroyos and were injured in falls. One died from eating poison weeds. One was killed by a mountain lion. Human members of the party dropped out, either from exhaustion or because the venture was far behind schedule. By the time the cape was reached only two people and five mules were left. The trip had taken half a year instead of the projected 14 weeks.

Mules and burros provide excellent transportation in otherwise impassable parts of the country, but there is no point in using them until you have to. Conventional automobiles sometimes survive Baja's rugged roads—but not always; the heat, dust, ruts and rocks take their toll. Cars or trucks with extra-low gears or four-wheel drive are more dependable. On recent trips I have used a four-wheel-drive station wagon with certain modifications: a variable pitch fan that cools the engine even when the car is traveling very slowly, extra leaves in the springs for greater load capacity and heavy-duty shock absorbers. I have also carried a large assortment of spare parts and the tools to install them, a second spare tire, two jacks and auxiliary gasoline tanks.

From the north, the most direct approach to Baja is through Tijuana and southward along the Pacific coast by way of Ensenada. There are almost 200 miles of good highway, and it is being steadily extended farther. The trouble with this route is that you do not begin to see what you are looking for—wilderness—until you run out of pavement.

I like to approach Baja through the other main northern gateway, Mexicali, located just over the border in the northeastern corner, because from that direction civilization is left behind much more quickly. Mexicali is a prosperous agricultural center and the capital of the Mexican state of Baja California, which covers the northern half of the peninsula; the less populous southern half is still federal territory. Completely modern, urban and progressive, Mexicali bears as little relationship to the country beyond as does Tijuana. You stop in Mexicali only long enough to pick up a free tourist card and in less than an hour you are in the desert.

A profoundly forbidding desert it is. To your left as you go south lies the present delta of the Colorado River, a tremendous alluvial plain that covers parts of Arizona and California as well as of the Mexican states of Sonora and Baja California. Some of it has been irrigated and cultivated, but on the journey south the green patches of irrigated land become fewer and give way to endless flats of dried mud and sand, scored by the river's many meandering channels. To your right is a spiky range of mountains, the Sierra de los Cucapás; beyond it lies Laguna Salada, or Salt Lake, which is no longer a lake but a flat 500-square-mile expanse of salty silt, generally bone dry except after a rainstorm.

The Laguna Salada, a sinklike depression that was once an arm of the Gulf of California and is now completely barren, is the most desolate part of the northeastern corner of Baja. Like so many other barren parts of the peninsula, it has a peculiar attraction for treasure hunters, lured by a story of a 16th or 17th Century Spanish explorer who is supposed to have sailed his ship into the Laguna Salada when it still contained water and was connected with the gulf. According to the account, his vessel, carrying a valuable cargo of black pearls from the lower gulf, went aground and was, in time, covered by drifting sand. The story is suspect. The lower gulf was indeed long famous for its black pearls; the pearl oysters began dying off only around 1940. But it is doubtful that the Laguna Salada has had water navigable by large ships since before the white man came. And if this foolhardy skipper had bags full of valuable pearls, what would he have been doing sailing around in shoal water instead of taking the deep-sea route back to Mexico or Spain to enjoy his wealth? Undeterred by such arguments, a small army swarms into the Laguna Salada every weekend to hunt pearls—people with hope in their eyes, greed in their hearts, shovels and electronic detecting gear in their jeeps and dune buggies.

The main part of the delta country is not quite as dry or forbidding as the Laguna Salada. One tributary of the Colorado, the Río Hardy, named for a British naval officer who explored the region in the 1820s, runs through this region. The delta also contains a number of small channels that on the map look like a bundle of nerves. There is not much left of the Colorado down near its mouth. Originating in the springs and snow-fed streams of the Rocky Mountains 1,400 miles away, it has been and occasionally still is a boisterous river, draining 265,000 square miles of the American West. In the area of the Grand Canyon it roars between steep-shelving banks and over boulder-strewn rapids. But dams and levees have tamed the lower river, and much of its flow is now siphoned off to provide drinking water and irrigation for Arizona and Southern

At the end of its 1,400-mile course, the Colorado River, by now primarily tidal water, flows gently into the northern end of the Gulf of California (top), considerably tamed since its headlong plunge through the Grand Canyon. Over millions of years the river has borne a rich cargo of organic materials to fertilize the delta soil and the gulf.

California. By the time it reaches its delta, the Colorado has become sluggish and unimpressive. About the only remnant of its former self is its color. The water, full of silt, is the dull red of old rust, the same hue that prompted the Jesuit explorer Eusebio Francisco Kino to call the river the Colorado—which is Spanish for red—during his 1701 expedition to the river's mouth.

The Gulf of California, into which the river empties, once extended much farther inland, covering Southern California as far as the San Gorgonio Pass, 200 miles from the present shoreline. The area now covered by the big Southern California lake known as the Salton Sea, whose surface is 279 feet below sea level, was once part of the gulf. But some seven million years ago the sediment-laden Colorado built a delta across this part of the gulf, leaving the Salton Sea area landlocked.

As you move south from Mexicali across this delta you are therefore traveling over the filled-in part of the gulf; a thick layer—three miles thick in some places—of silt, mud, sand and other detritus separates you from the ancient sea bottom. The flatness of the land promises to be endless; then, however, you sight the 750-foot-high Cerro Prieto (Black Hill), a mass of volcanic rock that juts up abruptly out of the beige and gray tones of the delta. This extinct volcano is not as out of place as it may seem. For just to the east of it lies an active volcanic field —called Laguna de los Volcanes, or Volcano Lake—erupting not lava but boiling mud and explosive steam.

These eruptions are external reminders of the subterranean violence that was the genesis of the entire peninsula as well as of its surrounding islands. Underlying the region is a continuation of the great fracture in the earth's crust known as the San Andreas Fault. Some 20 million years ago stresses and strains of the fault caused what is now Baja to begin to split off from mainland Mexico and also form the islands along Baja's shores. Since then, spurred by continuing activity in the earth's crust, Baja has moved obliquely northwestward some 250 miles, geologists estimate, and it is still creeping in that direction. This subterranean activity makes tremors common in the delta area and also accounts for the steam jets and mud boils of Laguna de los Volcanes.

A strong smell of sulphur assails the visitor; in some places the fumaroles scream like banshees. Pools of muck are tinted sulphur yellow, white or orange; some are the color and consistency of axle grease. It is a hellish scene, but it has its benign aspects. Baja Californians attribute great curative qualities to the hot mud baths. More important, the Mexican government is harnessing the steam geysers to produce pollution-free electric power. The steam-run generators will, they say, produce enough power to supply the northeastern corner of Baja.

Farther to the south the agitated landscape of Laguna de los Volcanes gives way to a more tranquil scene: the willow-bordered Río Hardy, which meanders toward the present mouth of the Colorado. At the mouth, the horizon is as straight and monotonous as a line drawn with a ruler. Some of the earth underfoot is marshy; some of it is cracked, dry, salt-coated mud. A few pilings near the mouth of the river mark the deserted site of La Bomba, once a small port. In the 19th Century, flat-bottomed steamers and barges that cruised the Colorado as far north as Yuma, and even beyond, took on cargo at La Bomba from shallow-draft seagoing vessels. This was the principal way of supplying the United States Army at Fort Yuma. But the railroad reached Yuma in 1877 and the waterborne traffic dwindled. Today it is difficult if not impossible for the smallest craft to navigate the shallow river.

With the reduction in water flow caused by dams and irrigation works upstream, another phenomenon of the delta has been impoverished. This is the tidal bore—which the Mexicans call *el burro,* or the ungovernable beast. Tidal bores occur in many parts of the world where large tides rush inland, creating a wall of advancing water. Tides in the upper part of the Gulf of California are enormous, ranging up to 30 feet. The tidal bore here was once especially dramatic because the incoming tides ran headlong into the swift current of the Colorado, creating a wall of water that moved upstream with awesome speed and destructiveness. When the bore formed it would, at first, be a stationary wave a few feet high. Then it would grow to a rolling comber six or seven feet high, rushing inland with great noise and turmoil. Behind the wave, water would spread out quickly over the flat land, with the level sometimes rising as much as 10 feet in five minutes. The bore inspired the early Spanish explorer Francisco de Ulloa, who reached the head of the gulf in 1539, to make one of the first sound observations about the region: "We perceived the sea to run with so great a rage into the land," he wrote, "and with a like fury it returned back again with the ebb . . . some great river might be the cause thereof."

The tidal bore caused puzzlement, consternation and occasional terror. In 1826 a footloose Missouri man named James Ohio Pattie was caught by it. He had trapped beaver on the Gila River, the Colorado's last major tributary, hacked canoes out of cottonwood logs to carry his pelts, and started down the Colorado hoping to find a Spanish settlement or trading center. He camped on the low banks of the great river and was overtaken by the tidal bore: "The rush of the tide coming in from the sea, in conflict with the current of the river . . . [formed] a high ridge of water, over which came the sea current combing down like the water over a milldam." Pattie's campsite was almost instantly under three feet of water; he lost most of his pelts and was lucky to escape with his life. It could have been worse. In 1922 a small steamer, one of the few that still attempted to enter the river, was overtaken by the bore. It capsized with a loss of 86 lives.

Not far from the Río Hardy is the Indian settlement of El Mayor. It is near here that the Sierra de los Cucapás terminates, and the Indians of El Mayor belong to a tribe named, like the mountains, the Cucapá. They constitute one of Baja's few surviving groups of aboriginal Indians. There are not many of them left in El Mayor and only a few traces remain of their primitive ways: rudimentary agricultural methods and huts made out of reed and thatch. More and more of them work at fishing camps on the Río Hardy or migrate to Mexicali for jobs.

In the past, however, the Indians of this area made a couple of impressive food-gathering expeditions each year across the desert wastes of northeastern Baja. One took them on foot over the dry, rocky Sierra de los Cucapás, across the desolate Laguna Salada and up into Baja's high mountainous spine to gather piñon nuts. The other expedition involved an even longer trek—almost 70 miles from El Mayor down to the fishing town of San Felipe on the Gulf of California—to dig for clams. The part of the desert they crossed on foot on these clamming expeditions is one of the bleakest on the peninsula.

Lying beyond the delta country and the southern end of the Cucapás range, this desert stretches almost unbroken for 150 miles down the eastern flank of Baja; some of it is a wide coastal plain and some a narrow passage between a succession of minor mountain ranges and the gulf. Much of it is totally bare although some parts, remarkably, sustain breathtaking stands of vegetation. There are occasional outcroppings of volcanic rock, alternately black and dull red, and high dunes, but the rest is rolling or flat and seemingly endless. A sun-blasted country of subtle colors, it is largely inhospitable but entirely fascinating.

There is an uneasy feeling of change and uncertainty—even danger —about the desert coast of the northern gulf. Twice each day huge tides race inland over the flats. Part of the sea water is lost to evaporation under the intense heat of the sun and the desert winds, and the flats are glazed with a blinding white rime of salt. The tides also constantly rearrange the shore, shifting mud and sand, polishing the stones, revising the shape of the headlands. This week's landmark may have disappeared by next week, or it may still be there in a wholly different and confusing guise.

At the head of the gulf the winds are almost as overwhelming as the tides. They race across the flats between mountains and sea as if through a funnel. Frequently the only moving things in this lonely landscape are the dust devils—whirling, whistling cones of dust and sand —that blow fitfully across the horizon. The constant scouring of the wind sweeps the sand along until there is an obstruction—a rock, a stick, a scrap of refuse. The sand piles up around the obstruction, which is soon hidden, giving the desert a clean, uncluttered look. Then the bulk of sand becomes an obstruction itself, and a dune may eventually be formed. But the wind gnaws away at the edges of the dune, restructuring it, and the dune is said to walk. Camping equipment left in the lee of a dune can disappear in minutes.

Sea storms are rare along this desert coast. But when they strike they do so with the fury of tropical cloudbursts, savagely altering the contours of the land. Rainstorms that would elsewhere be regarded as moderate, or even benign, generate flash floods here; the water runs too swiftly off the dry, unabsorbent soil. The desert earth is so poor in roots and humus that it is easily moved. Flood waters carve it into outlandish shapes—buttes, mesas and wide arroyos with their ancient stratification laid bare.

This is a country of baffling mirages. The air shimmers with the heat, and you travel in a sort of dream world between hallucination and reality. Ahead you see what appears to be a three-story house of strange conformation. It turns out to be a wrecked automobile at the side of the road. Off to the east you become aware, or think you become aware, of the gulf; a long promontory with clumps of trees or shrubbery extends out into it, enclosing a bay on which there are boats, some with sails. You are tempted to look for a turnoff, hoping for a place on the beach where you can rest and escape the terrible heat and glare of the desert. Your eyes search the roadside. When you raise them again the promontory is gone. The trees and boats, too. The horizon has changed utterly. Now there are four horizontal bands of color. Nearest is the monotonous tan of the desert; then a layer of blinding white, as white as new snow; then a band of indigo blue; then finally the paler blue of the infinite sky. But all of it is a little uncertain, dancing in the heat, and you wait for it, too, to disappear as had the promontory and the sail-

Rising abruptly from a silted plain near the U.S. border, the Sierra de los Cucapás rims the dry bed of the Laguna Salada (top left).

boats. But the colors are real. The dazzling white is the salt-caked coastal plain; the deep blue is really the gulf.

Your eyes return to the road. Ahead there is a series of black dots that seem to move in an irrational way, like a group of men trying to march along together but somehow unable to coordinate. You view this vista with skepticism. And when you get closer you see that the dots are another wrecked automobile, its parts scattered around, a door here, the hood there. Nearby are two cairns, each with a wooden cross and some faded paper flowers to mark the spot where someone died. This macabre scene, with its intimations of past horrors, recalls the way in which this particular stretch of wasteland got its name, El Desierto de los Chinos, the Desert of the Chinamen. The story is familiar; the tale varies with the teller. But roughly the facts are as follows.

Among the many Chinese who came to America in the 19th and early 20th Centuries to work as laborers was a group of Cantonese who settled in Mazatlán on the Mexican mainland around 1900. When work became scarce in Mazatlán they walked to Guaymas, 500 miles to the northwest; three of the group died on that trek. Again no work was to be had, so boarding a little steamer the survivors crossed the gulf to San Felipe in Baja California. San Felipe was a very small fishing village; here again there were no jobs for the luckless men. But they heard rumors of many jobs in Mexicali, 127 miles to the north; the canalization and irrigation work that was to make Mexicali a thriving oasis was already underway. The immigrant Chinese pooled their resources and paid $100 in gold to a man called José Escobado, who said he knew where there were water holes and promised to lead them across the desert to the border town. Forty-three men started out on foot to make the long trek across the desert. It was August 1902—and August temperatures in this desert can reach 125°F.

To say that the party was ill-equipped for any such venture is an understatement. The only water the men had was whatever they could carry in whiskey bottles or old oil cans. Many wore black smocks; dark-colored garments absorb heat. Some traveled barefoot and bareheaded —suicidal in such a terrain and climate. The sand and gravel underfoot are as hot as a stove lid. The body pours out perspiration in an effort to keep its temperature at near-normal levels. There must be an almost constant intake of fluids in order to avoid fatal dehydration.

The first water hole on the march was Pozo Salado, 30 miles from San Felipe. The next was Tres Pozos, another 30 miles beyond that. One marcher collapsed and died before the first 20 miles was covered.

The rest, aware now of their peril, tried to move on more quickly. But when they reached the spot where Escobado insisted the first water hole should be, it could not be found. Either his directions were wrong or the group had become confused by the shimmering mirages.

They pressed on. Other marchers collapsed and died, three of them in the salt flats near La Ventana. Only nine marchers were still with Escobado when he reached the spot where the second water hole should have been. Again, the water could not be found, and with this realization two more marchers gave up and died. Only Escobado and six of the Chinese managed to reach the Río Hardy, into which they collapsed after nine days of tortured wandering.

San Felipe, the Baja coastal village from which the Chinese laborers had set out, is 60 miles from the mouth of the Colorado; here the Gulf of California is 70 miles wide. The village is partially protected from the north by a rocky point that affords some shelter to fishing boats and shallow-draft vessels, although the tides, which here can rise and fall 22 or more feet, alternately ground and refloat those anchored near shore. Huge catches of shrimp and totuava are brought in here. The totuava, a specialty of the northern gulf, is a giant member of the weakfish family, running up to 300 pounds. It is highly regarded both as a commercial food fish and as a game fish, although wrestling one up from the bottom is more a feat of strength than of skill.

San Felipe is particularly exposed to gulf storms from the east and south. Several years ago the village was virtually wiped out by a *chubasco,* one of the intense tropical storms that periodically churn up from the Gulf of Tehuantepec far to the southeast. Rebuilt, it is now a popular sport-fishing center, operating on a year-round basis. Air conditioning, insulation and ice have made it tolerable if not luxurious. For those headed farther south it is the last reliable place to stock up on water, food, gasoline and other supplies.

From here on, the coastal desert is less traveled, because it is harder to negotiate. At intervals the rough road gets even rougher, dipping down into gravelly, rocky washes—arroyos that for a few hours in rare years are turbulent rivers bringing down the runoff from the mountains to the west. But most of the time they are only deep, dry scars in the landscape. Bad as the road is here, the shoreline is less forbidding. North of San Felipe the characteristic look of the gulf coast is one of salt-encrusted flats of sand and mud, but to the south there is a series of long, lovely sand beaches, separated by rocky points and isolated coves. You reach the beaches by following almost invisible tracks through the shrubbery of a chaparral wilderness, around dunes, between hills, along dry stream beds.

A few years ago my wife and I were lucky enough to visit this area in the early spring after a rainy winter. In this case "rainy" meant only a few inches of rain, but that is a lot in this arid land. Much as we loved the beaches, the country just inland was more interesting. For the dunes and arroyos were blazing with wild flowers: lavender sand verbenas, yellow poppies, stately white prickly poppies, delicate white desert lilies, owl clover, apricot-colored desert mallow and poisonous Jimson weed, which for all its noxiousness has a beautifully sculptured flower. We had known most of the desert flowers before, but here they seemed to bloom with singular brilliance. They may remain dormant through a succession of dry years. But then, encouraged by only a little rain, they explode with color.

A road of sorts follows the gulf shore as far south as Bahía San Luis Gonzaga, 225 miles below the United States border. But there is a certain monotony about the landscape and you find yourself more and more drawn to the high mountains that loom in the west. To reach them you retrace your steps back to the Valle de San Felipe, a broad, somewhat elevated desert. Near the point where the doomed Chinese laborers vainly hoped to find Pozo Salado waterhole, you turn inland.

Dry as the coastal desert is, this inland desert is even drier, for it lies just east of the high central mountains, which retain almost all the moisture that comes in from the Pacific. The desert flats and rolling hills are at first almost completely empty except for the scattered creosote bushes that invariably grow alone and widely separated. Here the shrub is called *gobernadora,* or "governess," presumably because of the way it dominates its immediate area. Natives say it poisons the earth, making it impossible for other plants to grow. This may be true, or it may be that the *gobernadora* can endure greater adversity than other plants. It clings to life in total aridity. Given a little moisture, its drab foliage will quickly change to rich green, with tiny yellow flowers. Its growth pattern is economical and tidy, and since individual plants tend to live separated from one another, the effect is a landscaped look.

From the Valle de San Felipe, the way leads across a broad, sandy wash called the Arroyo Grande. Along its borders there are a few small trees—mesquite, desert ironwood and shaggy-barked red shank, which the Mexicans give the more elegant name of *chamizo colorado.* These are apparently deep-rooted enough to tap whatever traces of moisture there may be under the dry wash. But on my last trip across the Arroyo Grande there was evidence of a recent shower. Yellow flowers bloomed on the low-growing brittlebush. There were also stands of a thin, delicate grass locally known as *finito.* It comes up quickly after a rain, quickly produces seed, then dies and just as quickly disappears, usually before any wandering range cattle can get at it.

Beyond the Arroyo Grande the desert is a little higher and a little better watered. There are magnificent stands of snakelike ocotillo; its multiple, thorn-clad stems, each tipped with a clutch of small scarlet flowers, etch intricate, graceful patterns against the cloudless sky. Succulents—plants capable of storing moisture—begin to be more plentiful. The most prominent are the thick-bodied barrel cactus and a variety of agaves, the spiky desert plants that are almost a cliché of the Mexican landscape. The big mescal agaves, which are common farther inland and at higher elevations, are abundant providers of food and drink. But the *mescalillos,* or little mescals, that you find here on the lower desert are of no known use except decoration.

The cholla cacti also begin to be abundant near the mountains. Neither useful nor decorative, they are the enemies of almost all living creatures. They are sprawling, untidy, thickly tufted with microscopically barbed spines of unmatched sticking power. I have spent tiresome hours trying to remove them from the soles and uppers of heavy field boots. One of the many species of cholla bears the specific Latin name of *molesta,* which seems more comprehensible than do most botanical designations. Nor is man the only victim of the molestation. I once found a cormorant, a large sea bird that had no business where I saw it, in the middle of the desert and miles from the ocean. It sat and glared as I approached, making no move until I was within a few feet. Then it struck at me with its long hooked bill, but made no effort to fly. It was crippled by a ball of cholla cactus caught in one foot, the spines sticking through the webbing. Gingerly wielding a shovel, I succeeded in prying most of the cholla away from the bird's foot, but it left many spines behind and the cormorant would not let me try to remove them. I had to go on, hoping that the bird itself would manage to pull them out.

A Canyon Oasis

PHOTOGRAPHS BY DAVID CAVAGNARO

Cañon Guadalupe is a bright ribbon of greenery that stretches up the flank of an otherwise arid mountainside in the Sierra de Juárez in northern Baja California. The cool, life-giving stream that creates this palm-shaded oasis flows down the fluted eastern slope of the range and plunges underground near the bottom of the canyon. It continues its subterranean course under a large dried-up lake bed that extends out from the mountains. Because of the stream, the canyon supports a host of plants and animals. And as an added bounty, in the lower part of the canyon hot mineral springs gush from the granitic rocks.

Since water is the treasure of Guadalupe, the best way to walk up-canyon is to follow the stream all the way to the waterfall at the Pool of the Virgin, a distance of about two and a half miles.

From the lush lower section where the walk begins there is a splendid view to the west of the two rocky spires that dominate the canyon. The more imposing is Picacho Rasco, which thrusts up about 4,500 feet into the cloudless sky. To its left is a smaller but more significant prominence that gives the canyon its name. For early explorers this slim pinnacle recalled Mexico's sacred Virgin of Guadalupe, and so the arroyo became Cañon Guadalupe.

To stand with a couple of companions in the lower canyon on a warm, sunny morning in February and to hear the gurgle of water brings a sharpened sense of pleasure. So does the coo of a white-winged dove and the insistent buzz of wings as a hummingbird makes its rounds. The desolate spires seem remote, the forbidding dry lake at the end of the canyon seems even more so.

This lake, called Laguna Salada, or Salt Lake, is a massive 500-square-mile depression that was once an arm of the Gulf of California. It is alternately a hard-baked salt flat and a shallow lake. Mostly dry since the mid-1930s, it continues to have one ironic connection with water: it serves as a roadway for tanker trucks that cart drinking water to Mexicali, the bustling border town about 35 miles to the north. The trucks raise great plumes of dust as they roar over Laguna Salada's flat surface to an isolated ranch where wells tap the cool water for Mexicali's tables—the same clear water that flows underground after leaving Cañon Guadalupe.

Palms dominate the lower canyon.

PICACHO RASCO AND (LEFT) THE SPIRE OF THE VIRGIN OF GUADALUPE

They crowd around the wide sandy stream bed, their tight clusters suggesting the scenery of tropical islands rather than sun-dried arroyos.

The palms are of two distinct types. Both are varieties of fan palms, so called because of the shape of their long fronds. By far the more numerous is the California fan palm, which is known to grow as tall as 60 feet. This palm, common also in Southern California and in Arizona, is quickly recognizable by the long curly fibers fraying from the edges of its fronds. The blue fan palm is the other canyon species, named for the bluish color of its fronds. Sometimes growing 40 feet tall, blue palms exist in the wild only in Baja California, although they are cultivated in many other parts of the world. They have been found as close as 15 miles south of the United States border, but wild specimens have never been seen on the northern side.

A Census of Palms

Recognizing the contribution of these fan palm species to Cañon Guadalupe's special ambience, an American writer and desert explorer named Randall Henderson once counted 1,155 palms in the canyon that were three feet tall or more. About 85 per cent, or some 980, were California palms. Since no one is likely to repeat Henderson's painstaking research, the total he arrived at remains part of the canyon's lore.

Handsome as they are, the California palms sometimes make the walk through the lower canyon difficult—and even noisy. As the palm fronds die they slowly wilt, the dry

A GROVE OF CALIFORNIA PALMS

remains hanging down the trunk. Over the years these dead fronds build up into thick sheaths or skirts. Walking among them involves pushing through the sheaths, which rattle and crash like sheets of metal foil.

On a bright February morning the noise seemed inordinately loud because the canyon was otherwise still, with one exception: an excited buzzing came from one small blue palm. Honeybees were swarming around its fronds—attracted not by the fronds themselves but by sugary secretions that had dripped onto them from some overhanging grasses. Little aphids with light green bodies and white hair-thin legs colonize these grasses, suck the juices from the stems and give off honeydew as a waste product. It is this that draws the bees—along with numerous ants. Some ants, wise to aphid habits, often corral colonies of these minute

A FAN OF PALM FRONDS

insects in mud-walled pens and carefully guard them—periodically harvesting the honeydew.

One of the bees seemed drunk with the honeydew. As it tried to fly off the blue palm frond, it keeled over and fell clumsily to the sandy canyon floor. It lay helplessly on its back, twitching as though in a death spasm until a helping finger flipped it onto its legs. After a few seconds of sporadic buzzing, the bee began to work its wings and soon rose slowly from the sand to drone off into the clear morning.

Following the stream along its luxuriant green bank, the hiker's steps frightened a tree frog that leaped away into a clump of grass. Though the adhesive pads on their feet enable them to climb easily, these little amphibians actually prefer hiding in rocks near the stream. Tree frogs abound in the canyon, but they are

APHIDS ON A WATERGRASS SHOOT

HONEYBEES ON A BLUE PALM

A TREE FROG IN GRASS

LADYBIRDS MATING ON A REED

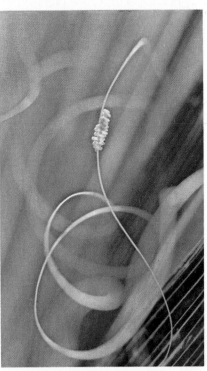

LADYBIRD EGGS ON A PALM FIBER

difficult to spot because they change color, blending into their surroundings of the moment—pale sand, greenery or the mottled texture of rocks. These sentinels of the canyon regularly call to one another, their resonant bleats sometimes the loudest noise in the air.

An attempt at close examination of the frog flushed from the streamside made it jump farther away. A hand extended to stop the jumping bothered the frog even more and it began to deepen in color. Soon the upper body was dark, perhaps from fear or frustration or anger.

On the stem of a common reed a few yards along, two ladybird beetles were mating. In another rite of spring, which comes early in Baja's desert, a female ladybird had already laid her eggs on a California palm frond fiber. This would seem to be a vulnerable place for the eggs, but they are always deposited near a food source. Ladybirds, especially as larvae, are energetic eaters of aphids, and these eggs were close to the aphids that were flourishing on nearby grasses. In fact, if there are no aphids available on which to feast, the ravenous ladybird larvae will devour each other. When the supply of aphids is exhausted or depleted, the ladybirds spread their wings and fly off in search of more food. Traveling in hordes that may number in the millions, they ride on the prevailing air currents for distances up to 80 miles. As they travel they live off fat stored in their bodies. If this food reserve is consumed and they find no new source of aphids, the ladybirds will starve to death.

Besides aphids, ladybirds eat a variety of other destructive insects including scale insects, corn ear and boll worms and mealy bugs. This habit makes them particularly valuable as a natural, nonchemical form of pest control. Farmers, managers of parks and gardeners now buy ladybirds by the gallon as predators of aphids and other insect pests.

Foraging along the margins of a still pool was a male giant water bug, its back covered with eggs laid there by the female. The male carries 100 or more eggs at a time, protecting them until they hatch, about a week after the female lays them. The giant water bug is one of several ferocious aquatic insects that live in the canyon's stream. A fearless predator, armed with a sharp beak, it will attack fish several inches long. More commonly—at least in the canyon —it eats insects and the pollywogs of the tree frog. Human bathers who have had the misfortune to tread too close to a giant water bug have learned the hard way why it is nicknamed the "toe biter."

The Demise of a Lizard

In a dry wash a few yards from the stream, a life-and-death struggle was unfolding so silently that it almost went unnoticed. In a tiny arena formed by an outcropping of rocks, a red racer snake had just captured a side-blotched lizard. This lizard, named for small dark blotches on its skin right behind the front legs, is common in the desert areas of the Southwestern United States and throughout Baja California. It eats scorpions, spiders, mites and ticks and loves to lie on rocks, basking in

A GIANT WATER BUG WITH EGGS

the sun. It had evidently been caught off guard by the red racer and was itself now being eaten alive. The three-foot body of the snake lay in sinuous loops on the sand. As the snake slowly devoured its prey, the lizard struggled in vain, bracing its rear feet against the snake's jaws. Its defense was futile. As more and more of the lizard disappeared, the movements of its rear legs were reduced to twitches.

The red racer seemed aware that it was being watched, but its meal was not yet safely inside. When it had swallowed all but the lizard's tail it glided with swift grace into the rocks, its tail tip vibrating so fast in alarm that it sounded like a rattler.

A RED RACER DEVOURING A SIDE-BLOTCHED LIZARD

CALIFORNIA PALMS AND COTTONWOODS IN THE MIDDLE CANYON

Although it is not poisonous, this snake is known for lashing out at intruders with its fangs. It is also exceptionally fast moving and adaptable; it can even climb a tree to escape an enemy. This red racer disappeared in a flash under the rocks. Behind it on the sand were only its tracks. No trace remained of the struggle—or of the lizard.

Bright Water, Fierce Beetles

On the way out of the lower canyon, the grade began to steepen. The stream bed was broken by small waterfalls—some miniature, others lazy, sprawling cascades that sometimes tumbled 25 feet. Between the falls, the stream meandered over the sandy bed in random curves and loops. There were occasional palm groves, with increasing numbers of blue palms. But cottonwoods and willows also thrived in the well-watered places between the rocks.

Though the canyon walls were closer and rose more precipitously here than down below, there was an air of openness: the vegetation was less dense, and fewer California fan palms towered overhead. The stream, which flowed rapidly over the rocks, was now a regular mountain brook, dappled with sunlight. The speckled granitic rocks were in places overlaid with colorful algae arranged in radiant mosaics.

Roots from the plants and trees that crowded near the sparkling stream often extended into the water. The roots of one willow tree streamed like long red banners in the rapid current, their bright color highlighted by the sun.

The steep climb and the warm sun induced a sharp thirst. A small waterfall seemed a good place to take a cooling drink. But the relief of water dashed over the face and filling the mouth was mingled with a sense of surprise. The water was peppered with tiny granules of sand. The swift-running portions of the stream keep its sandy bed stirred up. Carried by the water, the sand scours, polishes and erodes the rocks over which it passes until they are as smooth as sculpted ice. The sand grains were most unwelcome in the mouth; for a sandless drink, the canyon hiker must find a quieter, less turbulent stretch of the stream.

In the stream's more placid reaches the amount of aquatic insect life was astonishing. Under the surface of one limpid pool, the larvae of the predaceous diving beetle darted about busily. As its name implies, this beetle is an insatiable aggressor, a carnivore that preys on insects, snails, pollywogs and small fish. Even in its larval stage, this creature

A MOUNTAIN BROOK

PREDACEOUS DIVING BEETLE LARVA

is a highly efficient predator; to eat, the beetle grasps its victim with scimitar-shaped mandibles that not only serve as claws but contain tubes filled with digestive juices. The juices enter the body of the prey, reducing the tissues to pulp. The beetle then sucks the liquefied tissues back into its own body. The drained carcass of the prey is left to drift half submerged in the water.

A bit higher in the canyon, there was a good vantage point from which to look back down. In the middle distance, loose rock and soil that desert storms had washed down the canyon in huge quantities fanned out into the Laguna Salada; in the background the Sierra de los Cucapás rose bleakly from the flat desert floor. But here by the bubbling stream, the scene was anything but desolate; it teemed with life.

Not for long, however. As the climb continued, the stillness became palpable. The stream had disappeared—to flow underground. The high late-morning sun suddenly felt

ALGAE ON ROCK UNDER WATER

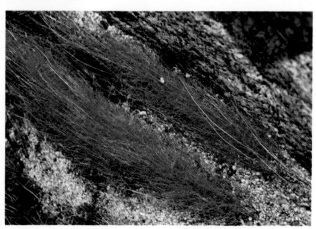

SUBMERGED WILLOW ROOTS

SPINY OCOTILLO STEMS

A PAIR OF MILKWEED CANES

BUCKWHEAT IN A CREVICE

particularly hot. Another backward look down the canyon drove home the uncomfortable fact that the vast desert is all-encompassing. Without water, no plant leaves or palm fronds rustled in the soft breezes, no frogs called, no doves cooed.

Yet in this arid higher section of the canyon, several types of creatures and plants managed to survive. Attenuated gray stems of the ocotillo sprouted from the dry slope, their long thorns arrayed in protective ranks. The desert milkweed canes looked dry and lifeless—as they do even when the plant is in bloom—but they were very much alive. With its whitish sap, milkweed is a favorite food of many insects, particularly the monarch butterfly, which lays its eggs almost exclusively on that plant. The milkweed canes were dotted with holes bored by beetles, another insect that relishes the sap.

In a tuck in the rocks, a delicate little buckwheat plant had taken root in a thin layer of soil. The fragile hexagonally patterned stems and the diminutive green leaves with their red trim were incongruously dainty in this rugged place.

Stark and vertical, the canyon walls were nevertheless almost gay with contrasting hues. The upper areas, exposed to sun and wind that had eroded the rock, were rust colored. The shadier lower portions were blue gray, decoratively threaded by light-colored veins that extended up to the higher canyon walls. These veins are scars created when pegmatite filled in the cracks caused by the cooling of the molten material that formed the mountain.

Near a barrel cactus and a stunted mesquite bush was a series of large, smooth holes—further reminders of the way wind and sand can erode rock. The process begins when a grain of sand or a pebble is caught in a rock crevice. As the wind blows, the trapped particle rattles around in the crevice. Continued over centuries, the abrasive action eventually scoops out a sizable hole.

Suddenly the stream reappeared —only to disappear again. This vanishing act was repeated several times, each disappearance abruptly recalling the desert.

Vague Menace, Then Clear Pools

In the climb up the inhospitable dry section of the canyon where the stream ran underground, it was all too easy to wonder if there really could be a waterfall at the Pool of the Virgin upcanyon. The feeling was akin to desert fever—a vague sense of doubt and menace. On that parched rocky slope, the vision of a high waterfall seemed impossible —even ridiculous.

But when the stream suddenly reappeared with palms and greenery proliferating near it, the feeling of uncertainty faded. A few sips of mountain water, drunk in the shade of a grove of California fan palms, were enough to make the earlier mood seem foolish. But the abrupt appearance of a stranger made it clear that the fever can infect anyone who walks the dry stretches of the canyon. He burst noisily through the palm sheaths, his face streaming with sweat, his eyes hesitant. "Is

BARREL CACTUS NEAR WIND-ERODED ROCK

there a waterfall around here?'' he asked plaintively. The answer was yes. In this pleasant grove near the murmuring stream it was hard to doubt anything—and certainly not the fact that the waterfall was just a few hundred yards ahead.

Upstream the rocks became boulders and some of the places where

canyon walls sprays of ocotillo and cholla cactus grew from invisible ledges where there was enough soil to sustain them.

Water striders scurried on the pool, their three widely placed pairs of legs distributing their weight so perfectly that they merely dimpled the water's surface. The strider's

breathing organs in their rear ends; while they can stay submerged for as long as six hours by breathing air they have stored in their bodies, generally they surface more often.

These back swimmers, which use their unusually long hind legs as oars to propel them around in the water, are yet another voracious water in-

A SHALLOW CANYON POOL

A WATER STRIDER DIMPLING THE SURFACE

the stream had worked its way between them were impossible to negotiate. Suddenly a wide, shallow pool opened up, fed by water tumbling down a rocky slope. The largest willow yet seen in the canyon arched over the sandy beach at the side of the pool, facing a magnificent cottonwood that spread its silvery branches across the water. Scattered palms graced the pool's edges, and high above on the sheer

middle legs propel it while the rear legs act as steering rudders.

Another type of strider, the riffle bug—so called because it is generally found near swift-flowing water —also darted on the pool's surface. The tension of the water was broken, however, by scores of insects called back swimmers. Swimming belly up under water, they occasionally stuck their bodies up into the air in order to absorb air through

sect. The pool was littered with the carcasses of their insect victims —both adults and larvae. Other remains, however, were casualties of the dangerous transition between water and air that various insects must make during their life cycle. The mayfly, for example, in its adult stages glides through the air on fragile wings, but in its nymph stage is aquatic. The fledgling mayfly sometimes comes to grief as it abandons its husk to fly into the air above the pond. New to flying, it may falter or be caught in a downdraft. If its wings hit the water and become wet, it cannot lift them to fly. Once trapped on the surface, it becomes easy prey —even for other mayfly nymphs.

To the Pool of the Virgin

Beyond the shallow pool, up the canyon, was the Pool of the Virgin. Dazzling in the intense midday sun, it was set in a large rock bowl under a slender 20-foot-high waterfall. Cottonwoods, willows and the ubiquitous palms grew around the bowl, and from its edges the canyon walls rose sheer, their flanks broken by growths of lacy green desert broom and *chuparosa,* a desert bush with a scarlet flower. Yet something was missing: it took a moment to realize that the pool contained no water. Instead, the Pool of the Virgin was full of sand. The waterfall once plunged into aquamarine water so deep that divers needed scuba gear to explore its bottom. Today it falls on the sand and snakes through a shallow channel to the former outlet of the pool. The present sand fill was the work of Hurricane Katrina in September 1967. This great storm sent floods pouring down the canyon, uprooting bushes and palms and carrying tons of sand that filled the bowl. Yet the slender cascade that once fed the Pool of the Virgin may be its salvation. Each year the falling water removes some sand, and if no future storm undoes its work, the chances are good that it will scour out the bowl and restore the Pool of the Virgin to its former deep, limpid purity.

THE POOL OF THE VIRGIN

3/ A Spine of Naked Granite

*Imbedded, the rock waves suggest a titanic storm
frozen to immobility. Isolated, the fragments...are the
giant headstones of the spirits of the mountain.*

GRIFFING BANCROFT/ *LOWER CALIFORNIA*

Viewed from the arid Valle de San Felipe, the abrupt scarps of the Sierra de San Pedro Mártir seem to be a wall of gray granite, jutting up almost vertically from the oven-hot desert floor. The summer heat of this particular desert valley is almost unbearable. When one day I remarked about the 121° heat, a resident told me, almost with an air of local pride, that on the same day the year before it had been 127°. In this heat it was hard to realize that by late October the nearby peaks of the San Pedro Mártir would almost certainly be covered with deep snow.

The highest of these mountains is Picacho del Diablo—Devil's Peak. It rises 10,154 feet into the deep blue sky, its rocky crest notched like a pale cockscomb. The east face of the mountain, and of the whole range, is scarred by arroyos and canyons that drop precipitously to the desert floor. These canyons end in great fan-shaped deposits of rocks and gravel, gouged from the mountains by torrents of rain or melted snow.

The Sierra de San Pedro Mártir and the Sierra de Juárez to the north of it are the highest ranges in Baja. Both these and the lesser ranges to the south form formidable barriers between the eastern and western parts of the peninsula, between the Gulf of California and the Pacific. In many places the mountains are impassable, in others cut by rough trails once followed by Indians and explorers and occasionally still used by ranchers and their cattle. There are only a few passes that a wheeled vehicle can negotiate. Travel in most of the peninsula is difficult. In this roughest part of Baja's rugged terrain, slow, struggling progress and long detours are the rule.

On a recent trip to Baja I decided to travel up into the mountains from the village of San Felipe on the gulf coast. The spurs of the San Pedro Mártir immediately inland to the west were impassable, so I headed northwest toward the San Matías Pass, which divides these mountains from the Sierra de Juárez farther north. Although I was moving into slightly higher elevations, the country was still arid, the vegetation still that of the desert—ocotillo, creosote bush, Jimson weed and many species of cacti. But here and there in the arroyos there was a hint of green, an indication of underground water and the promise of grass. The cattle from a nearby ranch, I had been told, were now in the high and grassy pastures of the mountains. They would be driven back down here for the winter, however; by that time there would be enough grass to support at least a few tough range cattle.

As I drove upward into the pass itself, I began to see more trees: cottonwoods and willows in the creek bottoms, scrub oak and pines on the slopes. The dominant pine was the Parry piñon, a tree that exists only in northern Baja and adjacent parts of Alta California. It is a species of pine that produces edible nuts, which grow in the interstices of the tree's egg-shaped cones.

The nuts provided a storable winter dietary staple for the Kiliwa and Paipai Indians, who once were numerous here in the mountains, as well as for the Cucapá from the Colorado delta. After gathering the cones in the early fall, the Indians would place them briefly in a wood fire to loosen the resin that held the nuts in place. Then they would grind the nuts into meal, using improvised metates—hollowed-out depressions chipped in flat-topped granite boulders.

The Indians also enjoyed an edible mescal that grows in the area of San Matías Pass and to the north in Valle de la Trinidad, baking the mescal hearts in a fire pit of white-hot stones. The three Indian groups of this part of Baja also had an abundance of seafood, brought up from the gulf coast, and game—birds, rabbits and deer.

There are still a few Kiliwa in the area, either working their own land or serving as cowhands on mountain ranches. They are a tall, strong people, good-looking and good-natured for the most part, but somewhat given to superstition. Any all-black animal is regarded as an omen of doom. Until recently, when a Kiliwa died tribal custom demanded that all of his or her possessions, including the house, be burned. The Kiliwa also believe in medicines that they derive from local plants. A tea made from the *canutillo,* a dry and brittle shrub, is thought to shrink varicose veins; the root of *yerba del manzo,* a weed gathered in stream beds, is considered equally efficacious for skin trouble in men and mules; the *senita* cactus is thought to have qualities that relieve stomach ulcers, as does rattlesnake flesh.

Driving into the ancient homeland of these Indians, I crossed through the San Matías Pass and bore to the south, toward the high mountains. Here the air was fresh and sweet—the piñon is a particularly aromatic pine—and the landscape became more grandly chaotic, strewn with gigantic gray, brown, dull red and white boulders. Some were in goblin shapes, some arranged in an intricate geometrical pattern like a castle built by a madman. But then the country leveled out into a series of magnificent and tranquil alpine meadows. There were parklike clumps of trees and rich pastures of wild grasses and clovers that flourish up here when the lower slopes and valleys are dry and bare.

In the desert few birds are to be seen—mainly buzzards, hawks, desert quail and a few fast-moving roadrunners. But here in the mountain meadows I saw mockingbirds, buntings, wrens, jays, quail, hummingbirds, wild pigeons and, now and then, ducks around the waterholes. There are animals here, too. Rabbits and jack rabbits abound, as do squirrels, ground squirrels and chipmunks, and there is an occasional Southern black-tailed deer. More secluded places are prowled by wildcats and mountain lions, although the latter have been hunted mercilessly and are becoming scarce. Mountain sheep, once plentiful, have also been shot in large numbers; small groups of wary survivors can sometimes be spotted through binoculars high up on the craggy eastern face of the mountains.

The pools, streams and occasional waterfalls of spring water in the high meadows contain one of the biological mysteries of Baja California: a small, brightly colored trout, similar to the rainbow but tentatively identified as a different species, *Salmo nelsoni.* Normally trout are creatures of the cool temperate zones and the arctic regions; how the *nelsoni* got to Baja is puzzling. Some local people believe that they were originally imported from Spain or from Alta California by missionary priests. This theory seems unlikely—how could they have been transported alive over such distances? Scientists disagree as to whether these trout belong to a distinct, endemic species or are merely rainbow trout that migrated upstream from the Pacific in an ancient time when Baja was better watered and its brooks more constant. Nowadays the many brisk little streams that originate in the San Pedro Mártir all disappear in the desert sand long before they reach the Pacific coast except in the wettest years, and even then their flow is brief.

The trout average about eight inches in length, although the largest ever taken that anyone knows about measured 22 inches. A friend told me that he had caught them merely by dangling a bright metal hook, unbaited, in the water. But when I mentioned this story to the game warden for the area he used the Mexican gesture of widening the right eye with forefinger and thumb, meaning "regard this with much eye," or "do not take it seriously." After wasting an hour in the Arroyo San Antonio fruitlessly casting a particularly seductive spinner, I was inclined to agree with him.

The higher country around and above the meadows is rich in vegetation. Thundershowers are fairly common here during the summer and early fall, and there had been one just recently. Lupine was blooming on all sides in many shades of blue. There were a few of the kind of penstemon I know as scarlet bugler—clusters of delicate deep-red blossoms at the end of long stems. Manzanita, with its contorted red-skinned limbs and gray-green foliage, was abundant; so were both purple and white sage. There were few piñons; they appear to prefer the more arid lower slopes. But there were other pines—sugar, pitch, lodgepole and Jeffrey—as well as willow, cottonwood, sycamore, aspen, fir, California juniper, incense cedar, live oak and an endemic cypress.

As the altitude increases the variety diminishes, and in the upper reaches of the mountains about all the trees one sees are the hardy Jeffrey pines, which thrive on dry, craggy slopes. Still higher, near the 10,154-foot summit of Picacho del Diablo, all is rock and, in season, snow. It is a peak accessible only to mountain sheep, birds and the hardiest sort of mountain climber. On the second highest peak in the sierra, 9,178 feet up, is an observatory built and operated jointly by astronomers from Mexico and the United States. The site was chosen after satellite photographs had shown northern Baja to be one of the three most cloud-free areas in the world (the other two are the west coasts of Chile and Africa). In order to carry in equipment to build the observatory, the University of Mexico broke 75 miles of road through the mountains and canyons from the Pacific side of the peninsula.

I wanted to see the observatory as well as the peak on which it perches, and so I drove south from the San Matías Pass until I picked up this newly made road. Grinding upward at about 10 miles an hour, I was stopped a mile from the observatory by a barrier in the road. Having gone to so much trouble to put their telescopes where the atmosphere is free of clouds, smog and "light pollution"—the glare given off by cities—the astronomers see no reason to allow dust-roiling vehicles to muck up their clear air. So I parked the car and walked the final mile —most of it vertical—gulping the thin air. The arduous climb was worth it. The observatory is impressive, but for me the view down was even more interesting than whatever could be seen by looking up. I found myself on the rocky brink of the eastern rim of the Sierra de San Pedro Mártir, looking down a mile and a half into the desert—into the dry arroyos I had crossed ascending into the range. After two days of travel, covering more than 100 miles, I had ended up only a few miles from San Felipe, where I had started. Off to the east it lay, looking even smaller than it actually is; and beyond it was the gulf, a glittering blue.

The visit to the observatory was all too brief, but there was another stop I wanted to make. From the base of the mountain it was but a few miles' drive by winding road to the Arroyo San José and a ranch owned by the Meling family. The Melings are one of the few families of non-Mexican descent that have managed to survive in Baja. They have done it through a combination of fortitude, intelligence and understanding of how to cooperate with a wilderness and not destroy it—a recognition of what a wilderness can be made to provide and what it cannot. Salve Meling, a native of Norway, came to Baja as a boy. Bertie, his wife, was born in Texas; soon afterward her father, Harry Johnson, moved his family to Baja. Johnson, a Dane, was one of the many foreigners, American and European, who settled in Baja in the last quarter of the 19th Century, drawn by the large land grants offered by the Mexican government and the high-pressure promotions of various land companies. Successive dry years in the 1890s were disastrous. Many of the newcomers gave up. Some, like Harry Johnson, survived for a time only by prospecting and mining. He staked a claim in the Arroyo Socorro, a gouge on the side of the San Pedro Mártir not far from the Picacho del Diablo. He then labored to build a primitive 18-mile-long earthen aqueduct that would bring in water with which to pan gold. Although the mine was a modest success, Johnson would probably have failed had not his whole family worked at growing food crops, raising cattle, making butter and cheese. Through prodigious industry and family solidarity they managed to be wholly self-sufficient.

Bertie Meling, now a high-spirited woman in her eighties, outrode seasoned *vaqueros* as a girl, outshot experienced hunters and once repelled a band of cattle rustlers singlehanded. Now she is the matriarch,

Baja's tallest peak, 10,154-foot Picacho del Diablo (center), thrusts its solid granite bulk above the pines of the Sierra de San Pedro Mártir.

not only of her own family but of a good part of northern Baja California as well—Mexicans, Indians and foreigners alike. She and Salve Meling and their family illustrate a truth about human life in this strange country. The peninsula's resources are meager. The impatient and greedy are quickly defeated, and the slovenly are lost before they start. But industry and patience, coupled with a respect for the land and its creatures, can bring a fair measure of success—if there is enough rain. Periodic rainless years have almost put even the indefatigable Johnson-Meling clan out of business. The long period of drought from 1949 to 1963 saw their cattle herd reduced from 3,000 animals to fewer than 150. But they managed to survive and even to laugh about it.

Early one day I took Bertie and Salve Meling up into the high country above their ranch for a view of the valley by morning light. Although there was little water in the Arroyo San José at this season of the year, its course could easily be traced by the green of the cottonwoods, willows and mesquites, and by the red roofs of the ranch houses nestled in the greenest part. But what interested me more was the behavior of my elderly companions. At the ranch they had been preoccupied with the dozens of problems that running a ranch involves and they had moved with the caution of age. But here on the heights they gamboled about like children on an outing, talking of the old days, the joys of taking cattle up into the high meadows for the summer and seeing them fatten, the quantities of cheese they used to make. Bertie bubbled with enthusiasm about undiscovered gold, about secret, magical places in hidden canyons, about some mysterious bones, discovered decades ago in one of these hidden places in the mountains, that she and others believe are the remains of a whale.

But with my companions' exuberance there was an air of prudence, too. As we walked to the edge of a granite cliff for another view of the valley, Salve would instinctively reach out every few steps and snap a twig of greasewood or manzanita. It was not to enable him to find his way back to the car; that would be easy. It was to make sure that if anything happened to us—a landslide, a fall over a cliff—the search party would be able to find our trail. Much as he loved the country, Salve knew its hazards and respected them.

At the Melings' ranch I picked up an old friend, Raul López, a civil engineer who has spent most of his life reconnoitering Baja in the employ of the Mexican government. Together we headed west, driving 25 miles to the Pacific coast, where we got onto the main road that leads south from the United States border to the town of El Rosario. This part of Baja is flat, uninteresting country, some of it irrigated land, much of it dusty prairie. At El Rosario we struck inland again. The road follows first one dry arroyo, then another, climbing steadily. Only a few hours from El Rosario we were back in an almost total desert environment, dominated by the strange *cirio* tree and cardon cactus. We passed an abandoned turquoise mine, made a side trip to a defunct copper mine and stopped to see the adobe ruins of the mission of San Fernando, the only mission the Franciscans founded in Baja California before leaving for the more promising fields of Alta California.

After driving another 18 miles up into the hills, Raul and I came out, finally, on a plateau that is known as the Llano de Buenos Aires (Plain of Good Airs) and traveled east across it. Despite its pleasing name, the plain is parched and uninviting. On our left the Sierra de San Pedro Mártir had diminished into a string of lesser mountains, little more than foothills. At the east end of the plateau we came to the ghost town of El Mármol, an abandoned onyx marble quarry.

Once El Mármol was famous for the density, beautiful veining and delicate coloration of the onyx it produced. Huge blocks of the stone were hewed out of the earth, trucked to the Pacific coast and shipped out of Puerto Santa Catarina. Eventually they were cut and polished for decorative use in courthouses, movie palaces, banks, temples and private mansions or, more modestly, were crafted into paperweights and inkstands. But for all the esteem in which onyx was once held, it has been replaced by cheaper substitutes, such as plastics, and El Mármol has been totally forsaken.

The hard, many-veined onyx is the product of a slow process in which a certain kind of heavily carbonated spring water creates stone by depositing layer upon layer of its minerals. The springs of El Mármol are still flowing, still making onyx. But there is nobody there to quarry it, or to cart away the cut blocks left behind when the place shut down. Big, rough chunks of colorful stone lie all about in disarray. Most of the quarrying and cutting machinery has been taken away, piece by piece. The town's dozen or so frame structures are mostly ruins; only two buildings remain, the one-room school and the one-room calaboose. Both school and jail were built of unpolished onyx marble blocks, orange, brown and white, solidly cemented together. Presumably they will be there forever.

We camped in the schoolhouse. Parts of the wooden floor and ceiling were missing and it was obvious that we were going to share the building with rats and mice, but this was preferable to camping outside in the cold wind that whistled through the ghost town. The night came quickly, moonless and clear. I got out my map and, by flashlight, studied where we were and where I had been and again was struck by the circuitous nature of travel in Baja California. We were, I discovered, at a spot some 90 miles south of San Felipe, the coastal village I had left four days before, headed for the mountains. There was no way, however, that I could have reached El Mármol directly from the gulf coast by car—the mountainous barrier in that direction is almost too rough for mules. So I had had to make an end run of some 275 miles, going north and west through the San Matías Pass, then south to the Picacho del Diablo area, then west to the Pacific coast and then southeast across the desert and up into the mountains again—all for a net gain of about 100 miles. This says something about the kind of obstacle the mountains constitute along the spine of the peninsula.

As we prepared to settle down for the night I asked Raul if he knew the rest of the poem that begins "I heard the trailing garments of the Night sweep through her marble halls!" He did not. They had not studied Longfellow in his engineering school. Raul is, of necessity, a practical man, but he also has a speculative turn of mind. "You know," he said, "if scientists ever find a way to turn stone into food, we in Baja California will be rich." Like many other Baja Californians, Raul regards his country with a mixture of love, awe, despair and hope: love of its rugged beauty and dignity; awe of its loneliness and dangers; despair at its hostility toward man; and hope that someday, somehow, it will become fruitful, productive, accommodating. And rich. The dream of riches, of somehow finding wealth in this stony landscape, has persisted in Baja from the time of the first white man to the present.

The most persistent dream—and probably the most fanciful—concerns the so-called lost mission of Santa Isabel and the supposed treasure hidden there by the Jesuit fathers. The story goes back to the unsuccessful effort of the Society of Jesus to civilize and Christianize the peninsula. The Jesuit order, always interested in remote and savage places, was authorized by the Spanish Crown in 1697 to undertake the job of settling Baja. During the next 70 years some 50 indefatigable, versatile Jesuit priests worked at establishing missions, planting crops and raising livestock wherever possible, and tending to both the physical and spiritual ills of the backward and recalcitrant natives.

It all came to naught. In 1767 the Jesuits were ordered expelled from Spain and all Spanish possessions, partly because it was suspected that the priests in their frontier outposts were enriching themselves at the expense of the state. This suspicion was the basis of the myth of the "Jesuit treasure." After receiving the news of their expulsion, the Jesuits in Baja supposedly gathered their treasure—gold and silver bullion, church ornaments and so on—and hastily built one last mission in which they hid it all. Estimates of the value of the legendary treasure range from $12 to $60 million.

Searches for the lost mission have come to nothing, but the stories abound. An airplane pilot, off his course in a storm, sights some ruins and a patch of green in a chasm but can never find his way back to it. A man stranded by a leaky boat on the desert gulf coast wanders inland; he meets an old Indian who has in his saddlebags a supply of fresh grapes and figs that he says he picked at a secret place back in the mountains, a place where there are the ruins of a house with a cross on the top of the adobe wall. A woman journalist from Alta California continues to hunt for the lost mission. She realizes that history and scholarship have established almost impossible odds against such a mission's ever having existed. But she enjoys the search and sustains her efforts with thoughts of Heinrich Schliemann, the German archeologist who was obsessed with the tales of Homer's Troy. History and scholarship were against Schliemann too, but he persevered and eventually uncovered the Trojan capital just about where Homer said it was.

But there are no Homeric tales of the efforts to conquer Baja California. The Jesuits' records tell only of their concern with nonheroic things—the cruelty and strangeness of the country, the difficulties of travel, the never-ending struggle to find water and produce food for themselves and their Indian neophytes. They were trying to create a frontier of civilization in an environment that promised little—and that gave nothing in return except emptiness and silence.

Man's Remnants Preserved

Every so often the traveler wandering through Baja's parched interior comes upon relics left by earlier visitors—missionaries and miners who, over a period of some 275 years, tried to make their mark on the country. The crumbling ruins of their houses, as well as their rusted machinery, have become an elemental part of the landscape, mute evidence of vain attempts to tame a gaunt and unforgiving land.

Today, although about one million people live on the coasts and northern and southern tips of the peninsula, the population of the central desert is not much larger than when a small group of Spanish missionaries arrived in 1697 in search of souls. The Indians they hoped to convert were nomads who left behind scant evidence of their marginal existence, but the missionaries—Jesuits, Franciscans and Dominicans—constructed buildings, irrigated the land and grew crops. For more than a century they explored and colonized Baja, and in the process established 30 missions. Even so they could rarely force more than a bare subsistence from the resistant land for themselves and their charges. By 1840, when they had all departed, most of the Indians, who had once numbered about 40,000, were gone too, the victims of civilization's diseases. All that remained there were the stone and adobe mission buildings that had been fashioned with the peninsula's own rock and clay.

In the late 19th Century other men were lured to central Baja to exploit its rich mineral deposits. Many towns sprang up and thousands of fortune seekers moved in to try their luck with promising lodes of copper, iron, onyx, silver, turquoise and gold. Some found wealth, but most found hardship and failure. Many lodes ran out, the terrain hindered transport, and the climate and shortage of water intimidated even the stouthearted. The occasional rock collector who now pokes around the deserted mines encounters little more than slowly healing scars of miners' tools, gaping holes and roofless houses (right).

Ironically, the extreme heat and desiccating air that work such hardships on man also serve to preserve his remnants. Gradually the adobe buildings, the wooden mine works, even the alien iron machinery have become more than relics. Protected by their isolation and transformed by time, they have become a feature of the Baja wilderness itself.

Decaying adobe walls offer a melancholy reminder of man's brief intrusion in the central desert of Baja. Standing in an overgrown arroyo near El Rosario, the walls were part of a dwelling probably built by early 20th Century miners working the nearby Sauzalito copper mine, now abandoned.

Drill holes stripe an outcropping of high-grade onyx at the deserted El Mármol quarry.

Abandoned machinery rusts at Calmalli, a mine that reportedly yielded $250,000 in gold.

Fortune hunters have long since left Desengaño, a gold mine in the central desert; a mine shaft now seems almost part of the terrain.

The adobe walls of the mission of Santa María de los Angeles slowly crumble into the earth from which they were molded by Jesuits in

1767. The ruins are in a steep-walled arroyo with a rare permanent water supply that still nourishes a cluster of stately palm trees.

4/ The Central Desert

*If beauty consists, as some say it does, in the
fitness of a means to an end, then the most grotesque
of the plants of Baja is also beautiful.*

JOSEPH WOOD KRUTCH/ *THE FORGOTTEN PENINSULA*

Most of Baja California is desert, and being desert it is a land of il-
lusion. From high places—such as the Sierra de San Borja, where the
Baja peninsula narrows to 40-odd miles—you occasionally can see both
the Pacific and the Gulf of California at once. Your eye is delighted
with the view of two of the world's great bodies of water and you are be-
guiled into forgetting that the miles between are long and painful ones.
The path to a clump of mesquite trees and a ranch windmill on the horizon, offering the promise of shade and water, looks smooth and easy;
but hours later—if you average five cautious miles per hour by car you
may be doing well—the oasis appears to be just as far away and the
trail has turned out to be all twists and turns, full of rocks, gaping holes
and deep sand. Not only distances are illusory; colors also change. The
wall of an arroyo glistens in the early sun with striations of rose, mauve,
greenish blue and sometimes the look of hammered gold—a magical
place. But when you reach it with the sun overhead the colors have disappeared and it is nothing but parched, bare, colorless rock.

The desert—any desert, and this central desert of Baja California in
particular—generates many of its own illusions, but man generates
many more. One of the most widely held is that the desert is a dead
and useless place, that what little life it supports is wholly inimical to
man: plants that bristle with thorns or spines or nettles; crawling, creeping, jumping creatures that can kill with a bite or sting. There are such

things, to be sure, and one is well advised to tread carefully. But this is a wide and empty country, and such encounters are rare. I once saw the tracks of a centipede in the dust of the Turquesa grade, so-called for an abandoned turquoise mine on the road inland from El Rosario. The tracks are unmistakable: parallel rows of closely spaced commas. I saw no centipedes, however, although I was always careful to knock my boots out each morning—the centipede's poison is not dangerous, but it is painful. I have seen only one black widow spider in all of Baja, at Rancho Santa Inés. Here there is a water spigot that the ranch owners graciously allow travelers to use to sluice away the desert dust. The spider, with its shiny black bulb of a body and the telltale mark of a red hourglass on its belly, had its filmy gray web stretched between water pipe and wall. I quickly finished my bath. The spider seemed wholly indifferent, content to remain in its cool retreat.

Scorpions, by contrast, are easily and frequently found, and in many varieties. One kind, seen on the island of San José, is more than six inches in length. Most scorpions are much smaller. They are among the most ancient of living things, little changed from the time some 400 million years ago when they emerged from the ocean and began living on land. Scorpions are not insects but the most primitive of the arachnids, a class that includes spiders and mites. They have external skeletons that they must periodically shed in order to grow, and lobsterlike pincers with which they seize their prey—small bugs mostly. For larger victims and for enemies (including man) they use the curved stinger at the end of their tail. The tail is arched forward over the back and the stinger is given a quick downward thrust, ejecting venom.

Suppliers of scorpions for venom research hunt them at night, using a black light that makes the scorpion's body glow. I have neither black light nor reason to collect scorpions, but I have no difficulty finding them in Baja. The scorpion does not stir from its hiding place until dusk —just the time when I am usually searching dry arroyos for dead wood or dried cactus to make a fire. Pick up such fuel with caution; hidden under or within it there may be a scorpion—black, sand-colored or reddish brown. Occasionally you find one that seems swollen, misshapen and almost white. Examined closely it will turn out to be a mother scorpion with several dozen tiny white baby scorpions riding on her back, and even these miniatures manage to look vicious. Fearsome as they seem, scorpions will retreat if they can; they will try to sting you only if they feel trapped. Such inoffensive creatures as desert mice and the elf owl regularly prey on them. Nevertheless, treat them with respect.

Deaths from scorpion stings in central Mexico—the venom can be fatal to children and persons in ill health—are said to outnumber deaths by rattlesnake bite by more than 10 to 1.

Regardless of the fact that scorpions are more common, the Baja traveler usually goes better prepared against rattlesnakes than against any other kind of menace. I do, even though I have seen more rattlesnakes within 20 yards of my doorstep in Southern California than I have in all of Baja California. You carry a snakebite kit containing a razor blade, suction cup and tourniquet. You wear heavy, loose-fitting boots and thick socks, and if you are very nervous you wear thick gloves as well; it is statistically true that more snakebites occur on hands and arms than on feet and legs. You usually carry whiskey, too, although it is useless except for solace and conviviality.

Some precautions are wise. There are 18 species of rattlesnakes in Baja. The commonest, the Lower California rattlesnake, *Crotalus enyo*, is found virtually everywhere in the lower three fourths of the peninsula—in the desert, in the mountains, along the seashore, on the islands, effectively colored and marked to blend with its surroundings. It is readily identified by the scaly mounds over its eyes that give it a beetle-browed look. In the northern part of the peninsula the red diamond, *Crotalus ruber*, also found in the southwest corner of Alta California, is common. One keeps one's ears constantly tuned for the warning buzz of the rattler when exploring in Baja. Having once been heard, this sound should be mistaken for no other. Even so, I have often mistaken other—and harmless—sounds for the one I did not want to hear: walking through dense brush or along a rocky stream bed and one terrifying time while lying flat on my back in a low cave in the Arroyo Cataviña looking at ancient Indian cave paintings on the ceiling. Always the sound turned out to be a pebble rolling or a cicada rasping or the wind rustling through a dry shrub. But even after you have sorted out the sounds in this almost silent world you often retain an uncomfortable question in your mind: what if the rattler did not rattle?

There is one rattlesnake in Baja California that does not and cannot rattle for the simple reason that it has no rattles. It vibrates its tail, as do many nonpoisonous snakes, and some say that there is a soft, whispering sound from the vibrations. But there is no true rattle.

This snake was first found in 1952 by a team of biologists who were collecting specimens on Santa Catalina, a small, uninhabited, mountainous island in the Gulf of California south of Loreto. The first one they discovered was a small but mature female, only 21 inches long, with colors ranging from gray brown to brown with cream-colored accents. It was, they decided, a new species and they gave it the name *Crotalus catalinensis,* for the island where it was found. In recording its characteristics, dimensions, coloration and scale arrangement, they noted that "no rattles have developed."

Laurence M. Klauber, who has written the definitive book on rattlesnakes, insisted that there was no such thing as a rattleless rattlesnake, unless it was the result of a rare deformity, an accident or maiming by a human being. But two more specimens of *catalinensis* were taken in 1962, and in 1964 a California Academy of Sciences expedition to Santa Catalina Island captured nine more. None had rattles. So it became apparent that on this one secluded island the rattlesnake had, through some strange evolutionary process, lost its most distinctive feature, the thing that sets it apart from the world's other snakes.

At various times man has supposed that the rattlesnake's rattle was used as a mating call, as a signal for other rattlers to rally and render aid in time of peril, as a "charm" to persuade birds and other edible creatures to come within range, as a way to shake poison dust in an enemy's eyes. All of these suppositions, while quaint, are false. The rattle serves as a warning, nothing more—a warning to frighten away whatever may be threatening the rattlesnake. Parts of an organism that lose their purpose or cease to function usually atrophy and sometimes are lost entirely. If this is what happened to the rattles of the *Crotalus catalinensis,* it raises some questions about the snake's habitat. Have its enemies disappeared? Man is a prime enemy and there are no men on Santa Catalina Island. But there are other uninhabited desert islands in the gulf and their rattlesnakes are of the conventional sort, with rattles. And the rattler has many enemies besides man. Some of them, notably hawks, are still present on Santa Catalina. Could it mean that the island's creatures exist in a sort of Peaceable Kingdom? Unlikely.

All that can be said safely is that *catalinensis* has, like many other organisms in Baja California, evolved in such a way as to be strikingly different from other species of the same genus living elsewhere. It has done so, probably, as a way of adapting itself to Baja's very special environment. Baja, in large part, is one of the most arid and forbidding landscapes on earth. The need to adapt to it has led to a high degree of local freakishness—or, to use the scientific word, endemism—among the flora and fauna of the peninsula. In addition the area contains many "biological islands." Some are islands in the literal sense. Others are islands in the sense that there are no easy routes to or from them; natural barriers enforce their isolation and guarantee the perpetuation of endemic types that develop in isolation. Leave one desert valley behind, cross a range of mountains and descend into the next valley—or row out to an island in the gulf—and you will find plants and animals similar to those you left behind but different in some specific ways.

There are, in fact, at least 28 such endemic species of mammals in Baja—to say nothing of birds, reptiles, scorpions and so on. Take for instance the jack rabbit. Anyone who knows anything about jack rabbits is aware that their coloration is protective. The shades of gray and brown of their coats usually blend perfectly with the landscape in which they live. But on the island of Espíritu Santo, in the gulf opposite Bahía de la Paz, there lives a jack rabbit that, in terms of color, makes no sense whatsoever. The island's landscape ranges from white to sandy to the dusty green of cactus to the dull red of an old lava flow. Yet the jack rabbits that occupy this island in considerable numbers are glossy black with cinnamon-red trimming on their ears and underparts, making them startlingly conspicuous against the low-key colors of their environment. Nobody knows why. Melanism—an excess of black pigmentation—occasionally crops up in various animal species, as does albinism, or lack of pigmentation. Did two melanistic jack rabbits occur in an original population of conventional jack rabbits and start a new race that survived and dominated because it was better adapted to life on the island? Or did the ancestors of this black race just happen to be on a piece of land that in the remote geological past broke away from the peninsula and became an island, leaving all the ordinary jack rabbits behind? Again nobody knows. But one thing is certain. The coloration is not protective, either from human or animal predators or the heat of the sun, which is intense in these latitudes.

Another bizarre Baja animal is a bat that is, to say the least, highly specialized. It lives in rocky crevices and shows a preference for islands of the gulf, as do many other bats. But while the other bats live on diets largely confined to insects, this bat lives on seafood. It skims over the water of the gulf at dusk catching small fish in its claws.

There are five endemic species of kangaroo rats—creatures with long hind legs that, like their namesake, travel by jumping. The kangaroo rats survive in a desert climate without drinking, at least in the conventional sense. There is a small amount of water in the plants on which the rat feeds. It eats only at night, when evaporation is lowest. When daylight comes the rat retreats to an underground burrow and

The isolation of stony Santa Catalina Island, 15 miles off Baja's gulf coast, has resulted in a unique species of snake, Crotalis catalinensis—the rattleless rattler. When frightened, it slowly waves its tongue and vibrates its tail vigorously, but gives no warning rattle. The knob seen at the center of the snake's coil is just a useless vestige.

sleeps all day; by this idleness it hoards the water stored in its body. It loses almost no water with its body wastes. This efficient system of desert living has its disadvantages, however. Because of its body-water content, the kangaroo rat is a prize morsel for many desert predators —kit foxes, snakes, carnivorous birds—that crave moisture but have not discovered how to conserve it the way the kangaroo rat does.

Baja has desert toads that hoard water even more carefully than the kangaroo rat. They spend much of their life underground in a state resembling death. But when a rain shower comes they awaken and dig their way up through the earth and into the fresh mud. They drink, eat and take their pleasure; then, as the desert dries up again, they dig their way back into their holes and return to sleep.

On some of the islands in the Gulf of California there is a giant chuckwalla lizard about two feet long. When fresh water is available the chuckwalla drinks it and stores it in built-in sacs, so that it gurgles when it walks. But when there is no fresh water, the lizard drinks salt water and puts it through what amounts to a self-contained desalination plant. Still another species of lizard—the worm lizard—has only two legs, both in front. The rest of its body is like a worm's, and it leads a wormlike life underground.

All of these creatures of Baja California are real. There are also some imaginary ones that exist only around campfires and wherever else tall tales are told: a giant man-eating gopher that seizes humans and drags them underground to devour; the *quileli,* a bird whose mournful cries are a sure omen of disaster and doom; another bird with two pairs of feet pointing fore and aft so that it can run in either direction with equal facility. But there are enough genuine mysteries without the imaginary ones. So many, in fact, that George Lindsay, director of the California Academy of Sciences and leader of many expeditions to the peninsula and the islands, has said that "for the scientist Baja California is a treasure chest, just barely opened."

Scientists trying, carefully and unobtrusively, to pry the lid open a little wider are found in the remotest parts of Baja California. Some of their pursuits seem to be almost of the needle-in-the-haystack variety. As one native commented, "They don't just study squirrels—they study the fleas on the squirrels."

The scientists come from all over—but not all of them look like wilderness researchers. Early one Sunday morning a few years ago I was waiting in the Tijuana airport for Francisco Muñoz, a bush pilot, to prepare his plane for a trip down the peninsula. While I waited, a pleasant woman who looked as though she might be headed for church—silk print dress, sensible shoes, white gloves, black straw hat—asked me to translate something someone had said to her in Spanish. She knew very little Spanish, she said, and she regretted it because knowing Spanish would be useful where she was going. It turned out that she, too, was flying on Muñoz' plane, destination San Ignacio, a small and isolated town about halfway down the peninsula.

Her name was Enid Larson and she was a high-school biology teacher. Her great interest was the coast chipmunk, a subspecies of Merriam's chipmunk. This particular subspecies is normally found only on the Pacific slopes of Alta California. But some 60 years before, a biologist named E. W. Nelson had found specimens of the same chipmunk in the mountains near San Ignacio, Baja California, about 500 miles from what had always been thought to be the animal's normal range. So this very ladylike biologist was going to plunge into the wilds of Baja California to see if the chipmunks were still there. She hoped to rent mules in San Ignacio and trek up into the mountains by herself. She had never been in Baja California before. She was excited, pleased with everything and astonishingly confident.

Muñoz took off with both of us aboard, and for part of the trip Miss Larson sat in the copilot's seat, exclaiming over the awesomeness of the Sierra de San Pedro Mártir, the beauty of the mountain meadows, the bright blue of the gulf, the seemingly endless stretches of sandy wasteland. When we reached San Ignacio, Muñoz first flew low over the town and its palm-lined oasis to alert the local taxi—a pickup truck. Then he buzzed the rock-strewn airstrip to frighten the goats out of the way. Only after these procedures, normal aspects of air travel in Baja, did Muñoz land. We unloaded the schoolteacher's bedroll, duffel bag, food, canteens and camera. Then we took off again, leaving her standing there in the desert in her Sunday dress, one hand shading her eyes from the sun, looking off toward the mountains and smiling.

Months later she wrote to me that it had made no difference that she knew so little Spanish. Everyone was very nice. She had rented her mules, had made her expedition up into the mountains and had later worked her way back down to San Ignacio over extremely rugged terrain. There Muñoz had picked her up again. Best of all, she had found her chipmunks, had become well acquainted with them, had learned a great deal and was delighted.

Part of the wilderness that supports Miss Larson's chipmunks and other strange creatures is empty and desolate: sweeps of plains and dunes, badlands and barren masses of rock that old desert movies— remember *Beau Geste?*—lead you to expect. But there are also parts of the desert that are almost parklike in their beauty. Strange shapes of black lava, gray and white granite boulders and rocks with a glittering patina of "desert varnish" (solar oxidation coats some rocks with a polished brown finish) thrust up cleanly out of gray gravel or powdery sand. The discipline and balance of their arrangement would satisfy a skilled Japanese gardener. Between and around them, and in some cases growing out of them, there is a bewildering variety of bizarre plants —cacti, yucca, agaves, ocotillo and elephant trees, and other thick-trunked, short-limbed trees that one early botanist described as being of dropsical appearance.

The cactus family is the largest and most diverse single group in the region. Cacti originally grew only in the Americas, although people have now managed to grow them in other parts of the world. In various forms cacti range all the way from Canada to the tip of South America. But Baja, central Mexico and parts of Peru and Chile offer the most variegated assortments. There are, in the Baja peninsula and on the islands of the gulf, at least 110 species of cacti, of which 60 are endemic. They range from buttons so small that they are easily overlooked to giants that dominate the landscape. Some are early forms in the evolution of the cacti, with woody stems and deciduous leaves. Some grow as stately trees, standing like sentinels in the lunar landscape of Baja's deserts. Others grow as vines and still others grow horizontally instead of vertically. The creeping devil, for example, can blanket the desert floor with a terrible tangle of spines as impenetrable as barbed wire.

Cactus spines range from stiff, needle-sharp spikes that can easily pierce a boot or automobile tire to tiny hairlike glochids that penetrate the skin and disappear like invisible splinters. They are all weapons that the various species of cactus have developed to protect themselves. Some cacti are edible and animals would wipe them out were they not armored with protective spines. Other cacti sometimes claim victims that have made no attempt to eat them. On the coast near El Rosario I once saw a petrel that had evidently chosen to nest in a clay bank that was well concealed by long-spined cholla cacti. It had doubtless seemed a safe haven. But the petrel, probably trying to escape from a predator, had apparently tried to fly into its burrow at top speed. The bird hung there dead, impaled on the cactus' vicious spines.

Not all cacti are so fiercely armored, but all have one feature in common. The mark of the true cactus is the areole, a pad or cushion in the stem, corresponding to a bud on the stem of a more orthodox plant. The areole is usually covered with a soft feltlike material and out of it grow the spines. If the cactus produces leaves, and some of them do —usually small, insignificant and short-lived—the leaves will often grow out of the stem just below the areole. Most cacti, however, lack leaves and this, together with the normally bulky construction of the plants, provides a vital defense against aridity. With no leaves and only short stems, the expanse of plant surface exposed to the air is considerably reduced—and so is the loss of precious moisture through evaporation. The thick, waxy quality of the cactus' skin also helps to conserve water.

The king of the cacti is the cardon. It is frequently mistaken for, or confused with, Arizona's magnificent saguaro. But the cardon is a distinct—and larger—plant, found only in Baja California and a part of Sonora, across the gulf in mainland Mexico.

The cardon has a short, treelike trunk, sometimes as much as five feet thick, out of which grow towering fluted columns, soaring upward, sometimes erratically but most often with the symmetry of candelabra. The cardon is said to reach a height of 60 feet. The largest one I have ever seen, in Baja's north-central desert in the Arroyo Cataviña, which the cardon shared with a beautiful stand of blue palms, was just under 50 feet. I calculated its height by the old-fashioned method of matching shadows, which is easy in the uncluttered desert. I am six feet tall and my shadow measured 10 feet. The cardon's shadow measured 80 feet. Elementary algebra says that if a 10-foot shadow is thrown by a six-foot object, then it must be a 48-foot object that casts an 80-foot shadow.

The only other true giant of the central desert is the *cirio,* one of the weirdest members of the vegetable kingdom. While not as massive and monumental as the cardon, it grows even taller, sometimes reaching 75 feet. It is a relative of the ocotillo—both belong to the candlewood family—but it resembles little else in the real world. With its slender, tapering tip pointed toward the sky, it has often been compared with a giant carrot growing upside down. The *cirio* frequently abandons upright growth, however, and bends itself into arcs, loops and question marks. A grove of *cirios,* particularly if silhouetted against the sun, looks like a wholly disorganized group of eccentric dancers. Where its neighbor, the cardon, is majestic, the *cirio* seems almost silly. It is a prolific inspirer of whimsy. It has been likened to Medusa of

Bristly fruits and withered blossoms adorn the tops of a small species of cardon. The fruits are inedible, but they make fine hairbrushes.

the snaky locks and to a teenager with unmanageable arms and legs. One of the first botanists to study it was so astonished by its strangeness that he nicknamed it the "boojum" after the mysterious threatening creature in Lewis Carroll's great nonsense poem "The Hunting of the Snark."

Many of the trees and shrubs that share parts of Baja's central desert with the cardon and the *cirio* have a strange foreshortened appearance. Some are large and some are small, but all have thick short trunks and stubby writhing branches—a type botanists call sarcocaulescent, or fleshy-stemmed. These fleshy stems enable the plants to soak up and retain what little rain falls in this superarid part of the world. The contortions of the branches are somehow reminiscent of Laocoön and his sons and the trouble they had with serpents. Casual observers tend to describe them all as elephant trees—because of their bulk, their dry, smooth, paperlike bark and the fact that the branches are frequently as sinuous as an elephant's trunk. In fact they belong to three different botanical genera—*Pachycormus, Bursera* and *Jatropha*. The *Pachycormus discolor,* known colloquially as the *copalquin,* is large and showy. When it blooms it produces an unbelievable mass of small but brilliant pink flowers. The *Bursera,* known locally as *torote,* is usually somewhat smaller; when it blooms its cream-colored flowers are very small and unobtrusive. The *Jatrophae* are shrubs, smaller still, and are known to natives as *matacora* and *lomboi*. Like many other desert plants, both the trees and shrubs of this thick-stemmed group bear leaves only briefly, thus reducing the area exposed to the drying air. In addition, the plants protect themselves against grazing creatures by producing an aromatic sap that the animals find distasteful—but that Baja natives use as medicine. The sap of the *lomboi* in particular is valued as a curative ointment. One old rancher claims that as a boy, about 70 years ago, he suffered badly from chapped lips—a common complaint in desert country. But, he said, one application of *lomboi* sap cured the chapped lips for all time; he has not been afflicted since, although he has spent his entire life in the desert.

The various agaves, or "century plants," notably the mescal, are especially useful—as food, drink and even shelter. Unlike the cacti, which store water in the stems, the agaves store water and food in their thick leaves and in the artichokelike heart where the leaves are joined together at the stem. When full grown—it takes a long time but not, as the name implies, a century—the plant sends up a tall, rapidly growing stalk. At the climax the stalk produces flowers and seeds. In this final

A slow-growing plant that blooms only once, an agave, or mescal, shoots up the tall stalk of blossoms that signals its death. The energy for this fatal flowering comes from nutrients stored in the plant's low-lying rosette of overlapping leaves. The leaves, thick and tough, can be processed and made into twine, sandals and roof thatching.

burst of energy all of the agave's reserves are used up and, having flowered only once, the plant dies. But before blooming and dying the agaves, and particularly the mescal, can be bountiful providers. The heart of the plant, shorn of leaves and buried underground with white-hot stones, is cooked into a sweet and nourishing vegetable. The plant's stored water can be drunk fresh, fermented or distilled. If the rapidly growing stalk is cut off before it reaches the flowering stage, the sap that the plant produces to support this rapid growth collects where the stalk has been cut. It is sweet and potable and is known as *aguamiel,* or honey water. Distilled, this sweet liquid becomes the fiery liquor called, like the plant itself, mescal.

The most popular sources of food in the desert are the pitahaya cacti. Both sweet and sour varieties nourished the Indians, cured early explorers of scurvy and are still eagerly harvested by Baja dwellers. Mesquite, regarded as a pest in some cattle country, is considered a friend in Baja California. Both it and the desert ironwood retain their leaves longer than most desert plants and provide shade for humans and food for grazing animals. Both trees are good for firewood. With its yellow sapwood and dense brown heartwood, desert ironwood was particularly valued as fuel for wood-burning steamships when they plied Baja's waters. Indians harvested the seeds of both trees as a storable food. Animals like the seeds, too; the cracking of mesquite and ironwood seeds by mice and rats is one of the night sounds of the desert.

Other edible seeds come from catclaw, goat nut, *palo verde, flor de San Miguel,* various desert grasses and, of course, many of the cacti. In some parts of the desert the Indians ate flowers, including those of the ocotillo, the herblike greens of purslane, mustard, saltbush and salicornia, the dates of native palm, wild plums and figs. The wild fig tree, whose roots spread over rocky terrain like melted candle wax, is one of the handsomest botanical sights of the peninsula.

These resources are meager in comparison with those of better endowed parts of the world. Still, they offer a slender margin between life and death in the desert, if there is a little water. Given sufficient motivation, energy and ingenuity, man can adjust himself to such a stringent regime and can find enough food to support life, both for himself and a few cattle. Beef—cut in strips, salted and dried in the intense sunlight—becomes jerky. Salt is plentiful, thanks to the great evaporative salt beds on both coasts, and it is used in preserving both meat and fish. Soft boots, called teguas, are fashioned from deerskin. Cowhide becomes saddles, harnesses and the voluminous leather skirts that are used to protect both horse and rider in thorn country. Rawhide is an all-purpose fastener and is braided into *reatas,* or lariats, the basic tool of the desert *vaquero,* or cowboy. Dyes for cloth and leather come from fruit, bark, roots and seeds.

Some people have managed to survive and thrive on these slender resources of Baja's central desert. But many more have tried and given up. When ranches, mines or missions have been abandoned, domesticated animals frequently have had to be left behind, and some have reverted to a wild state. There are a few wild horses and many wild cattle. Except for the fact that they lack a brand, the wild cattle are difficult to distinguish from those that are owned by some rancher; both types are scrawny and spooky. Every five years or so ranchers from all over Baja gather in the vicinity of El Arco and stage a roundup of wild unbranded cattle.

Then there is the wild burro. To appreciate this beast you have to know the domestic burro, surely one of the saddest, most ill-treated and overworked of animals. Although slight, burros are remarkably sturdy and sure-footed. They can carry tremendous loads through boulder-strewn arroyos, along ribbon-wide terraces above canyons, through deep sand. They can go for long stretches without water and eat the roughest sort of forage. They are slow, sometimes recalcitrant, and are beaten regularly because of it. The domesticated burro seems to withdraw into itself. Its eyes are dim, resigned. Its long ears lie back or flop forward limply, its coat is usually filthy from rolling in the dirt to ease aching muscles and pack sores.

Wild burros, however, are something else. I had heard about them before I ever saw them. Ranchers turn their mares loose on the range to breed with the wild jacks—male burros. The mules thus produced are thought to be particularly hardy. Sometimes wild burros are trapped. A fresh waterhole is dug in a stream bed and the wild burros are lured in by the smell of water. They are captured, chained to logs and left until they are near starvation. Their captors then bring them bundles of twigs and leaves from the *dipua* tree, a relative of the *palo verde,* which the burros love. Within a few days they are seduced into tameness, and within weeks they can be broken to work—far more quickly than a mule or horse. And sometimes they are hunted—although many Mexicans refuse to eat burro meat. On its withers the burro is marked with a cross of darker hair. It is said that this is a badge of divine protection, granted to the burro for its services in carrying Mary and the Christ child on the Holy Family's flight into Egypt. An engineer from Santa Rosalía told me that he had once gone deer hunting and, failing to find any deer, had shot a young burro. He dressed it and cut out a fillet of loin, which he then took home and gave to his cook. The cook said the meat looked too dark for venison and the engineer told her it was antelope. She then used the loin to prepare *albóndigas* (meatballs), and both she and her employer agreed they were very good. Some days later the engineer overheard the cook and a friend discussing with horror someone who had not only killed a burro, but also eaten its flesh, something that they would never do. With an impulsiveness he later regretted the engineer said, "Ah, my good cook, but you have eaten burro. You remember the antelope . . .?" The cook left the house, never returned and never spoke to him again.

On a recent trip to Baja I was told that there were many "savage" burros in the Sierra de la Asamblea and the Sierra de San Borja to the south of it. I began seeing them in the pass between the two mountain ranges that leads down to the gulf port of Bahía de los Angeles. The burros were usually in groups of three. I saw my first group shortly after passing an abandoned gold mine fittingly called Desengaño, or Disillusionment. They might well have been descendants of the burros that once hauled ore from the mine to a mill at Las Flores. They were sleek and clean, apparently well fed. Their eyes shone, their ears were alert, and they made me think of the prophet Jeremiah's description of wild asses that "snuffed up the wind like dragons." They would allow me to approach on foot within 100 yards; then they would move off at a brisk trot, eyes still on me, ears pricked sharply forward. Freed from servitude, they were wholly unlike the poor beaten-down domesticated burro. They had gained both strength and dignity in the wilderness.

A Garden of Implausible Plants

As a visitor moves southward in Baja, the vegetation he encounters becomes, like Alice's Wonderland, "curiouser and curiouser." Pine trees and other familiar plants gradually give way to exotic species, formed and structured by millennia of isolation and extreme aridity. In the sprawling deserts that dominate the southern four fifths of the peninsula, many of the species are so bizarre as to stir awe and disbelief.

Fantastic plant forms—growing sometimes in patches, sometimes in whole forests—give the landscape a surreal, dreamlike look. Immense cardons, the world's tallest cacti, lift their columnar arms to bewildering heights, dwarfing the gnarled branches of 20-foot-tall tree yuccas. A creeping devil cactus inches its spiked, wormlike stems over rock and earth. The tall, sinuous *cirio* often shares rocky slopes with the squat, massive elephant tree, and by this proximity each accentuates the other's peculiarity.

Strange though they may seem, all of Baja's plants are magnificently adapted to withstand the heat and drought that are their lot. The cardon cactus, for example, is essentially an enormous, expansible water-storing organism that without benefit of leaves carries out photosynthesis—a plant's sun-powered food-making process. The *cirio*, or boojum, defies drought by lying dormant during the long dry months; it springs to life, putting out minuscule leaves, during the desert's brief periods of rainfall. Scores of other desert plants have their own special mechanisms for collecting and conserving the precious moisture.

While such adaptations are not unique to Baja, many of Baja's plants are themselves unique. In the cactus family alone, 80 of the peninsula's 110 species grow nowhere else on earth. Of about 40 large plant families that have been identified in Baja, many are represented by only a single genus and often by a single species, indicating a limited range of evolutionary responses to the region's rugged environment.

The peculiar attractiveness of Baja vegetation is just as compelling for the scientist versed in its botanical eccentricities as for the uninitiated layman. The eminent naturalist Joseph Wood Krutch once recalled that even on his tenth visit to Baja he was in "a state of high elation," finding that "the scene was weird even to one by now accustomed to the usual desert weirdness."

Brilliantly highlighted by the evening sun, a remarkable grouping of oddly shaped plants juts up from a slope near El Rosario. At left stands an enormous cardon cactus; another, at right, looms above a barrel cactus, while a third cardon, to the rear, is flanked by a pair of polelike cirios with dried flower stalks on their crowns. Just below at center is a five-branched senita cactus. The low clumps in the foreground are a species of the fiercely spined cholla.

Responding to summer heat and drought, an elephant tree slips into dormancy. Soon its leaves will fall, baring a labyrinth of branches.

A Ponderous, Paradoxical Tree

A vision of grotesque splendor, the elephant tree is one of the strangest of Baja's own species. With a short, ponderous trunk and fat, contorted branches that taper abruptly into a maze of dry twigs, the tree rarely grows as high as 12 feet. Yet some elephant trees spread their branches over an area 40 feet in diameter.

Despite a desiccated appearance, the elephant tree copes well with its desert environment. During the long months of heat and drought, it stands dormant—barren and seemingly lifeless. Then, in the wake of a rare desert rain, it bursts into a mass of tiny bright green leaves—which make photosynthesis and growth possible. From time to time, the paper-thin outer skin on trunk and branches cracks and peels off to reveal a spongy blue-green inch-thick inner bark that covers the tree's pulpy water-storing core.

Before retreating to dormancy, an elephant tree may make a last gorgeous gesture. Almost overnight, the branches become decked with pink or red blossoms. While in bloom —usually for a period of only a few weeks between May and September —the tree is transformed into an ineffably light and charming bower; the effect is spectacular, especially when a cluster of flowering trees is glimpsed unexpectedly in the distance. But as a tree lapses into sleep, it again takes on its more familiar aspect: an outlandish tangle of brittle twigs and elephantine branches.

Pleated branches rise from a cardon cactus.

Stately Giants of the Desert

In every particular, the cardon cactus inspires awe. Seen growing as a forest in the distance, the leafless giants look like ritual obelisks left behind by an elegant vanished civilization. Seen singly close up, they have an air of confident strength. The largest specimens may be 200 years old and 60 feet tall; they may weigh 10 tons—and may even double that weight when their widespread roots sop up the rainfall of an explosive desert storm.

The cardon owes its tremendous capacity for absorbing water to a thick spongy interior and a flexible pleated skin, both of which easily expand and contract. The cardon's great bulk is supported by long hardwood rods that grow inside the raised ridges between its vertical pleats. Lacking leaves, the whole green plant does the work of synthesizing the organic materials required for life and growth.

Each spring the cardon puts forth a scattering of fragrant white flowers that bloom at night near the top of its columns. After several days the flowers fade and the plant produces round golden fruit with close-set tawny spines. Baja's Indians once gathered the fruit for its seeds, which they ate toasted or ground into meal. But the most useful part of the plant is the hardwood supports inside its columns. The rods are so strong yet so supple that they serve equally well as rafters, fish spears, fence rails and bedsprings.

Hundreds of cardon cacti, some with columns 60 feet tall, set off a dense forest (foreground) in the bleak hills near Bahía Concepción.

The Tortuous Tree Yucca

Rough-barked and gnarled, its bent branches reaching skyward from its upper trunk, the tree yucca is a familiar sight in the vast sandy regions and gravelly slopes that occur over much of the Baja peninsula. Although its average height is about 20 feet, specimens as short as 10 feet or as tall as 25 are not uncommon; their trunks may be almost two feet in diameter. The growth of this hardy member of the lily family depends in part on local conditions of wind, water and soil. In the foggy valleys of the Vizcaíno Desert (right) the moisture-laden winds favor the tree yuccas, which dominate the neighboring cardon cacti. Farther south, however, on stretches of the Magdalena Plain where the climate is drier, the cardon instead overshadows the tree yucca.

Everywhere it grows, the tree yucca shares a symbiotic relationship with the small white night-flying yucca moth, each ensuring the other's survival. The female moth collects pollen from one of the tree's white dill-scented flowers, which emerge in spring in a cluster from the big clump of narrow leaves at the end of each branch. The moth rolls the pollen into a tiny ball and deposits it, along with its eggs, inside another blossom. About half of the seeds produced by this pollination nourish the moth's hatched larvae. Of the seeds left uneaten, a few manage to take root in the soil and grow into mature yuccas.

Tufted tree yuccas, sharing a Vizcaíno valley with cardon cacti, bend and sway in the wind-swept fog that rolls in from the Pacific.

An assortment of cirios flaunt their whiplike branches in curves, loops and arches.

A Skinny, Sinuous, Spiky Species

In Baja's vegetable kingdom, the *cirio,* or boojum, is the court jester. It stands ludicrously tall and thin; the largest specimens rise 60 feet from a base measuring no more than two feet in diameter. Most *cirios* of whatever height look as branchless as broomsticks, although some, apparently in reaction to injury, develop sinuous arms that grow in every imaginable shape. All *cirios* bear their pale yellow blossoms in an improbable nosegay at the very top of the slender trunk.

The key to survival for many desert plants is their compact moisture-preserving form. But the ungainly *cirio* fares perfectly well despite its inefficient shape, thanks in part to the thick waxy skin that covers its trunk and branches. Throughout the worst of the desert's incessant heat and drought, when the *cirio* is standing dormant and leafless, its skin seals in moisture, which the tree preserves in its pulpy interior.

In the rare times of soil-soaking rainfalls, the *cirio's* sharp-spined branchlets quickly put forth tiny bright green leaves, and within a day or two the tree is photosynthesizing at full speed. When this supply of moisture is used up, the *cirio* drops all its leaves, thus effectively reducing the surface area that is exposed to evaporation. Once more naked and dormant, the tree is again dependent upon its waxy exterior and spongy interior to help it subsist until the next rainfall.

Soaring skyward, a majestic 30-foot cirio sports five main branches and scores of branchlets, many of them still bearing faded leaves.

Sweet pitahayas stand in slanting clumps near the Pacific coast in southern Baja. Plants of this species often grow to 15 feet or more.

Forests of Sweet and Sour Cacti

The most important sources of fruit in Baja are two species of cactus misleadingly known by the same name, pitahaya. The two plants are hardly look-alikes: the so-called sweet pitahaya puts forth a tall, symmetrical cluster of branches (hence its alternative name, organ pipe cactus), while the sour pitahaya is lower and pricklier, and sends its stems sprawling in wild disarray (hence its popular name, galloping cactus).

Botanically, the two species are less closely related to each other than the sour variety is to the creeping devil cactus (*overleaf*).

On the other hand, the fruits of the pitahayas are not the opposites that "sweet" and "sour" suggest. Both have a fragrant, refreshing pulp that is cool to the tongue on a hot day. The sour variety is slightly more acid, and most travelers prefer its tartness to the bland sweetness of the other variety.

Not so the Baja Indians. They prized the sweet pitahaya so highly that they reckoned time by its fruiting season, June through August, calling the period "the Time of Pitahayas." During those months, one account records, the Indians enjoyed endless pleasures: "There was no hunger and little work. Young and old thronged our thorny forests, eating juicy, ripe, red pitahayas as large as a horse's hoof; eating and drinking continually; sleeping when tired of dancing, and eating again as the languor of sleep passed."

Sour pitahaya stems, alive (rear) and skeletal.

A Crawling Cactus with Devilish Armor

The creeping devil or caterpillar cactus is a sinister-looking plant whose fiercely barbed stems crawl slowly but relentlessly along the desert floor. As each stem elongates with new growth—it may reach a length of 10 feet and a thickness of three inches—it puts down roots at intervals and crawls over any obstructions, be they rocks or other creeping devils. Meanwhile, the older growth gradually withers and dies.

Freed from the parent plant, the stems become new and independent plants. They in turn proliferate by sending out stems of their own as well as by the usual production of fruit and seeds. Multiplied by the death of the old as well as by the birth of the new, creeping devils often form a huge tangled colony with stems radiating in all directions from a ring of withered plant tissue.

How far will a creeping devil creep? Actually, not as far as it may seem, for two practical reasons. First, the species' growth rate is limited by severe aridity to less than an inch a year; second, its range has been curtailed (and its survival threatened) by the spread of irrigated farmlands on its native Magdalena Plain. Yet theoretically there is no limit to the lengths to which a creeping devil will go. "Conceivably," says botanist George Lindsay, "one plant could grow forward for centuries, dying off behind as it progresses, covering many miles and achieving a kind of immortality."

Inching outward from dead and dying tissue, barbed stems of the creeping devil cactus colonize a stretch of the Magdalena Desert.

5/ The Glistening Gulf Coast

*Then the sea/ And heaven rolled
as one and from the two/ Came fresh
transfigurings of freshest blue.*

WALLACE STEVENS/ *SEA SURFACE FULL OF CLOUDS*

After long days and nights in the central desert of Baja, no matter how much you may love that beautiful, ghostly landscape, there is something restorative about coming through the mountains and seeing the Gulf of California spread out to the horizon, blue and glistening. The life of the desert is subtle, unobtrusive, motionless. By contrast the sea always bears the promise of abundant life and change.

From the desert the way to the gulf leads between the tangled ranges of San Borja and Calamajué and then down to the beach at Bahía de los Angeles, an isolated fishing settlement about a third of the way down the peninsula. These normally drab mountain passes can, after a rain, explode with flower colors: purple verbenas, golden poppies, white evening primroses, masses of yellow flowers on the *palo verde* trees and clouds of pink blooms on the elephant trees. But most of the time this high country is dry, bare and brown. Here as elsewhere on the eastern side of Baja, the mountains shut off the westerly winds and whatever moisture they might bring from the Pacific. But at the base of the mountains at Bahía de los Angeles there is a dependable spring of sweet water surrounded by greenery. Nearby are shell middens—piles of ancient sea shells—indicating that for at least 6,000 years man has either lived or camped here, enjoying not only the trickle of fresh water, but also the wealth of food that comes from the gulf. Clam and scallop shells are everywhere, as well as the carapaces of giant sea turtles.

Bahía de los Angeles has a small but secure natural harbor, the only one in a 150-mile stretch of inhospitable central gulf coast. The harbor is bounded on the north by a long sandbar that is partially submerged when the tide is high, and on the south by a headland. It is shielded from the open gulf by an outlying barrier of islands. With this protection from the sea and a supply of fresh water, Bahía de los Angeles is a snug refuge. People seeing it for the first time occasionally lament the waste of opportunity. It could be a thriving seaport, bustling with shipping, or it could be a great modern resort. And perhaps if it were located in a more accessible part of the world it would be. But like most of Baja it is difficult to get to and therefore remains an oasis of quiet calm. There are only a few native people and only a few visitors at any given time. Some of the natives are commercial fishermen; the bay and the gulf yield up excellent scallops. But the bulk of scallops is so slight, once the shells and viscera have been cut away, that a few light planes suffice to haul them to market.

Otherwise there is little traffic. Small ships and pleasure and sport-fishing boats occasionally drop anchor in the bay, but they hardly ruffle the settlement's slow and easy pace. The only place a visitor can stay is the modest hostelry run by Antero Díaz, a gracious, hospitable man whose wife, Cruz, serves ample meals of fish, clams, scallops and lobster. Díaz' ways are so relaxed that his guests are expected to keep track of how long they have stayed and how many beers they have fished out of the cold box.

It is the offshore islands that give a special character to Bahía de los Angeles. This is the narrowest section of the Gulf of California, sometimes called the waist, sometimes the midriff, 70 miles wide and dotted with 50-odd islands, some large, many no more than rocky pinpoints in the sea. From here on south to the tip of the peninsula one is seldom out of sight of islands. And in time there may be more islands. The central gulf is an area of geological unrest; earthquakes could thrust the summits of submarine mountains above the surface of the sea to become new islands.

The largest of the islands on the Baja California side of the gulf, 10 miles offshore, is Angel de la Guarda, or Guardian Angel. It is 42 miles long, and some of its peaks are more than 4,000 feet high. It is uninhabited and, since it has no water, uninhabitable. Seri Indians, a tribe with an old—and perhaps deserved—reputation for cannibalism, sometimes came there from their home on Tiburón Island to fish and hunt turtles, but they do so no longer. There are stories of Angel de la Guarda's serving as a hideout for desperate men, but such tales are suspect. There are equally remote places that would be more comfortable to hide in than this sun-blasted mass of arid sand and rock.

In the narrow waist of the gulf, the flow and ebb of tides, running into or escaping from the upper gulf, cause great currents and eddies. The currents run at speeds of five knots and more, making navigation difficult for experienced skippers and almost impossible for novices. In many places surface upwellings bring cool water surging from the bottom, adding to the turbulence. All of this agitation ensures a high oxygen content in the water and maximum movement of microscopic plants and animals, the smallest but most important links in the sea's food chain. The result is an almost unmatched variety of marine life.

Through the channels that run between the Baja shore and the gulf islands, and between and around the islands, there are frequent processions of whales. While humpback and sperm whales are often sighted, the commonest species in the central gulf are the finbacks. Finbacks are streamlined monsters, second only to the great blue whale in size. They range up to 75 feet in length, up to 80 tons in weight. Like all baleen whales, the finback feeds by straining sea water through the comblike arrangement of whalebone in its jaws, filtering out small crustaceans and other sea creatures as well as plants for food. The gulf finbacks travel in pods ranging from a few whales up to several dozen, but they apparently do not travel far. They seem to prefer to stay in the gulf rather than to roam the oceans of the world as other whales do. Specialists have estimated that there are perhaps 250 of these nonmigratory whales. Some believe that, in times past, finbacks found their way into the gulf and never found their way out. Others think that the richness of the food resources of the central gulf makes it too attractive for them to leave.

When I approached Bahía de los Angeles for the first time I stopped, sat in the shade of an ironwood tree and scanned the horizon with binoculars. I hoped I might see a pod of finbacks, but could find none of the telltale spouts. However, I found compensation in the spectacular view of the islands from the slight rise on which I was stationed. Though they thrust boldly up from the bottom, from this vantage point the islands seemed to float on the water in a shimmer of opalescence, their colors shifting from misty blue to white, from gray to tawny brown, from mauve to dull red, depending on the angle and intensity of the light. It was late August; while the sky over Baja was brilliantly clear. the mainland side of the gulf was having a summer storm. Great thunderheads were piled up on the horizon; there were flashes of lightning and that peculiar clarity of light that frequently accompanies a storm.

Confident that it would not rain on my side of the gulf, I slept on the beach that night and in the morning was rewarded with one of the gaudiest sunrises I have ever seen. The rising sun glared angrily from between the lingering clouds, beating a brilliant red and orange path across the gulf, outlining the dark islands with a rim of fire.

There were still no whales, but there was proof of the food richness of the gulf in the gathering numbers of sea and shore birds as full daylight came. Brown pelicans patrolled the beach, seemingly awkward, lazy and indifferent. Nearby, gulls marched up and down. On rocks and pilings black cormorants sat, wings outstretched to dry in the early sun. High overhead floated frigate birds with their widespread, graceful wings and long forked tails, motionless against the morning sky. Then at some unseen, unheard signal the birds took off, the gulls and cormorants swiftly, the pelicans as cumbersome as overloaded airplanes. Far out on the gulf there was a riffle of silver, and here the birds headed. The cormorants formed undulating black ribbons against the sky, the pelicans a stately single file. Schools of small fish were being driven to the surface by larger fish below—as these may have been driven by still larger fish from greater depths. The pelicans circled the area of activity, fishing on the edges, raising their beaks to let the fish slip headfirst down their throats. The cormorants plunged into the water, sleek as arrows. The gulls—the noisiest of the lot—wheeled and fluttered over the water, snatching fish, flying again, quarreling over their catches. And the frigate birds, which cannot swim, flew low to try to rob other birds in flight. It was a dizzying spectacle, an explosion of bird life as dozens of fluttering, crying, fighting creatures dived and battled and screamed and flapped furiously.

A ramble south along the bay shore, part sand and part rocks, turns up other evidence of the marine life of the gulf. As you walk above the tide line you disturb hundreds of tiny hermit crabs, each carrying its borrowed shell on its back. Beautiful Sally Lightfoot crabs, their red, blue and brown shells gleaming like baked enamel, seem to skim across the sand and rocks on tiptoe. All along the beach there are many shells that have either washed ashore or been left there by a human or animal predator: murex, scallop, snail and clam, including the big *hacha,* or hatchet, clam, the muscle of which, seasoned with lime juice and eaten raw, is a great delicacy.

Below the tide line there are pools with hundreds of tiny fish, so small that they are barely visible. There are some skeletons of larger fish that have been stripped clean by minute marine scavengers, the isopods and amphipods. In deeper pools you find starfish, spiny purple sea urchins and green-flecked sea cucumbers. On the rocks close to the low-tide mark, where the water occasionally washes over them, are algae-eating limpets, looking like elongated bone buttons. Nearby, chitons creep along the rocks, their armor-plated bodies looking like headless, legless miniature armadillos.

On the sand, where low tide has exposed a green, oozy carpet of algae and plankton, there are veined olives—snails with elongated egg-shaped shells speckled brown on white. They eat their way across the green carpet leaving a clean, narrow path behind them. Turban snails, some brown, some white, some olive green, live on the same forage. The shells of turban snails, when vacated by the original occupant, are highly regarded as housing by the hermit crabs.

For an even better view of the marine life I like to visit the sheltered coves along the rough coast between Bahía de los Angeles and Bahía las Animas, the next bay south on the gulf. Here, swimming with a face mask, I can examine clouds of unidentifiable but brilliantly colored tiny fish and armies of small herringlike fish known here as *sardinas*. Beyond them, in somewhat deeper water, are flashing hordes of silver mullet and darting schools of torpedo-shaped sierra mackerel, polka-dotted yellow and blue. Garden eels, their tails sticking down into their burrows in the bottom, wave in unison like flower stalks in a breeze. Barred grunts stir up the bottom with their undershot jaws. Beyond these, numbers of green jacks can be discerned patrolling the outer limits of shallow water, driving the smaller fish inshore. The green jack is known colloquially as the *cocinero,* or cook, presumably because its herding activity provides so many fish for Baja tables.

Of the 586 known species of fish in the gulf, all but about 10 per cent are found close to the shores of either the peninsula or the islands. But since these inshore waters quickly drop off to depths of 100 to 500 fathoms, virtually all of the gulf's fish can be found within sight of land, including big sea bass and giant groupers, some of them a drab brown and gray but one kind a brilliant golden yellow. Also swimming close to shore are such large members of the jack family as the yellowtail, the roosterfish and the jack crevalle, as well as the most beautifully rainbow-hued fish of them all, the dorado, or dolphin. Why they are called dolphin is a mystery, for they are no relation to the true dolphin. But

A school of goatfish, one of hundreds of species found off Baja's gulf coast, swims in sun-dappled shallows near the island of San José.

the name is ancient, its first recorded use being by Sir Francis Drake's chaplain in 1578. They are memorable fish because they turn every color of the rainbow when hooked, landed and dying, evidently because of upheavals in the organs and chemicals controlling the color cells. The most famous description of this peculiar phenomenon is by Lord Byron: "Parting day dies like the dolphin, whom each pang imbues with a new colour . . . the last still loveliest."

Also to be found in the gulf are giant manta rays, shaped like great kites, 15 to 20 feet wide and weighing a ton or more. For all their sinister appearance and gross size, manta rays are harmless creatures —although the small sting ray that lies on the bottom in shallow water can, if stepped upon, inflict a painful wound by means of a poisonous bony spine on its tail. The manta ray's distant relative, the shark, however, is far from harmless and there are many of them in the gulf.

Colloquial Baja names for the various sharks tend to be confusing, as they are almost everywhere in the world. Some are not hard to translate, however. The shark the Baja natives call the *cornuda,* or "horned one," is, of course, the hammerhead, a dangerous creature with eyes on the extended lobes of its mallet-shaped head. The *tintorera pinta,* or "spotted shark," is, logically enough, the beast known in English as the leopard shark, while the *tintorera barcina*—*barcina* means dappled—is the tiger shark. But the native name for one species of shark, *sardinero,* or "sardine eater," tells us nothing, since all sharks prey on small fish. This brownish shark, along with the *cornuda,* is valued by the native fishermen for the size of its liver.

At one time shark fishing was a brisk industry in the central gulf and farther to the south. Although many North Americans scorn shark meat —and the ancient Greeks thought eating it produced melancholy—it is not only nourishing but can be delicious if properly prepared. In the Orient it is considered an aid to longevity and sexual potency. In Latin America it often passes for bacalao, or dried codfish, a staple of Lenten diets but also eaten the year round.

In the 1940s there was a boom in shark fishing in the Gulf of California as well as along much of the Pacific coast. German occupation of Norway early in World War II shut off the world's greatest source of cod-liver oil—valuable because of its vitamin A content. But it was found that the livers of some sharks produced 100 times as much vitamin A per gram of oil as cod livers. In some Gulf of California communities virtually the entire male population took up shark fishing. Chains and huge hooks baited with chunks of meat would be towed by two men in a dugout canoe. The hooked shark was killed by blows on the head, towed ashore and cut up at a favored butchering place like Carmen Island, some 230 miles southeast of Bahía de los Angeles. The liver was packed in large tins. The fins and edible flesh were cut off, salted and dried in the sun. The head, the tough hide and the cartilaginous skeleton were left for the carrion eaters. One shark butchered on Carmen Island had a liver so large it filled five five-gallon kerosene cans —at a time when shark liver was bringing four dollars per pound. The entire fish—liver, meat, fins and all—turned out to be worth $720.

The boom ended when synthetic vitamin A was developed in the late 1940s. The people of Baja still go shark fishing, but in a minor way; the monetary inducement is no longer very strong. Two men working a dugout together may, if they are lucky, catch 15 sharks in a week-long trip. For these they will divide about $50. Their activity does not make much of a dent in the large shark population of the gulf.

I have fished the midriff section of the gulf from a party boat, but much as I like to fish, I am more fascinated with the local bird life. The islands of the gulf are even more isolated than the peninsula, and some of them are almost exclusively bird islands, with either permanent or migratory populations. Some islands are dominated by a single species. Robert Orr, associate director of the California Academy of Sciences in San Francisco, estimated the 1966 brown pelican population of Patos Island, which is on the eastern side of the gulf near mainland Mexico, at between 50,000 and 100,000, and it was only one of the many islands on which pelicans congregated.

Some of the other birds cruise the oceans of the world, only rarely resting on a beach or promontory. Then, as the breeding season approaches, they return to the same small island in the Gulf of California where they know by instinct they will be comparatively free to nest, lay their eggs and hatch their young.

San Pedro Mártir Island in mid-gulf belongs primarily to the boobies —so-called presumably because their behavior has given people the idea that they are stupid. They do not look it. Both the brown booby and the flashier blue-footed booby are big, handsome birds with fierce eyes and a crew-cut top knot. Boobies are strong fliers but are often robbed of the fish they catch by the bigger frigate bird. Either bravely or foolishly—perhaps this is the true source of the name booby—they seem unafraid of man, often allowing him to approach within a few feet of their bare rock nesting sites. Their young are hatched black and nearly naked, but quickly develop a coat of thick white down, so thick that they sometimes appear almost as large as the adult bird.

Many of the birds of the islands are small and inconspicuous—certainly less conspicuous than the pelicans and boobies. The petrels are small—both the black petrel and the even smaller least petrel—and they lack color, but they make up for these deficiencies by the beauty of their flight. They hover over the water, seeming to dance on the surface. Then, at the slightest disturbance—they are very shy—they dart away in flight that matches the grace of a swallow and the speed and unpredictability of a bat. The petrels nest in rock crevices, burrows and holes. They may be neighbors of another burrow dweller, the murrelet. Murrelets are small relatives of the auks and puffins and are about half the size of the common murre found in northern waters. Two species are found in Baja California—although they are so nearly alike that ornithologists have trouble differentiating them. The Xantus's murrelet (named for János Xántus, an eccentric Hungarian naturalist who was an observer of Baja wildlife in the 19th Century) is found on the islands off the Pacific coast of Baja. Craveri's murrelet—named for another 19th Century observer, the Italian meteorologist Federico Craveri—nests and hatches its young on the gulf islands. The murrelets are oceanic voyagers during most of the year, but they return to these same islands year after year to nest and lay their eggs. The eggs are large ones, considering the bird's tiny size, and the female never produces more than two during any nesting season. The parents take turns sitting on the eggs. But the murrelets do not favor life on land. As soon as nesting is over and the chicks are able to swim and fly, the birds resume their seagoing travels.

The activities of such small birds as the murrelets are furtive almost to the point of being imperceptible. By contrast, the breeding and nesting activities of the larger, more aggressive birds on Raza Island are not only obvious but spectacular. Raza, the only mass breeding ground for Heermann's gulls and elegant terns, is a tiny guano-coated island, no more than 250 acres in area and 100 feet high, with a sparse cover of sage and saltbush. It is about 35 miles southeast of Bahía de los Angeles, one of a series of tiny islands between the big islands of Angel de la Guarda and San Lorenzo. If you are lucky enough to be in this area in April—one of the pleasantest months of the year on the peninsula—get Antero Díaz to take you from Bahía de los Angeles to Raza by boat to witness what must surely be one of the strangest sights in na-

A relative of the gannet, the clumsily built blue-footed booby sometimes seems to have been created only to amuse onlookers, especially when it lurches along on its large webbed feet. But it gives a superb performance at sea, where it may swoop from 100 feet in the air in pursuit of its fish meals.

ture, territorial war without end. Such wars go on between many species, but they are rarely so plainly seen as on Raza.

The island offers a breeding and nesting area not only for Heermann's gulls and elegant terns but also, to a lesser extent, for the royal tern. All three are handsome birds. The Heermann's gull is medium-sized, 18 to 20 inches long, with a dark gray body, black tail, white head and red beak. Like most gulls, it is noisy, belligerent and voracious. It ranges along the Pacific coast from Central America to British Columbia, spending much of its time on the water, resting briefly on beaches.

Both the elegant and the royal terns have white and pearly gray bodies, black-crested heads, and beaks ranging from yellow to orange. The elegant tern is found as far south as Peru and Chile, as far north as San Francisco. The royal terns—a distinct minority—are almost as large as the gulls; the elegant terns are somewhat smaller.

In February or March the terns and gulls begin their annual pilgrimage back to the Gulf of California. They sometimes nest on other small islands, but Raza is their principal target. The gulls arrive first, breed and scratch nests out of the soil. The nests are crowded, separated by only 18 to 36 inches. I have flown over the island in mid-March, the beginning of the nesting season. Even this early, and viewed from an altitude of a thousand feet, the gulls appear to have occupied every square foot of the island.

Then the terns arrive. At first they only feed and preen themselves. Then one night, set off by some mysterious signal, they take to the air and hover in a dense and noisy mass over the already nesting gulls, driving them from their nests. Many of the terns alight, scratch their own nest basins and immediately lay eggs. Tern nests are even more densely crowded together than those of the gulls, in many cases less than a foot apart. By daybreak the terns have established a beachhead—usually a tight-packed circle, perhaps 30 feet in diameter. But then the gulls counterattack. Stalking among the terns, they frighten the interlopers into the air and begin eating the tern eggs out of the nests. If a female tern refuses to leave her nest, a gull will merely push her off or even spear an egg out from under her. The gull pecks the tern egg open and eats it on the spot. By evening the terns' 30-foot-wide nesting ring has been reduced by perhaps half, although within that smaller circle they continue to sit on their nests. Then during the night a fresh wave of terns attacks again to re-expand the perimeter of the tern beachhead. They repeat the previous night's performance, hovering noisily over the gulls and driving them off. Again the terns alight and lay eggs;

by morning the circle is perhaps 40 feet across. With daylight the gulls again attack, but the crop of tern eggs that survives the onslaught is larger than before. Each night the terns extend their limits. Finally they may have a dense colony spread over an acre of land, and there may be several colonies on the island, each surrounded by angry gulls.

The tern eggs in the center of the colony hatch first. When they can walk, the young terns tend to congregate along one edge of the colony. The gulls now alight in the resulting cleared area and attack the terns and their eggs from within the colony as well as from its outer boundaries. But somehow, despite all the mutual hostility, the terns manage to raise enough young to perpetuate their species. So do the gulls, although the terns' occupation of their nesting ground and the continuing warfare have reduced their egg crop, too.

Forty or so years ago the seasonal gull and tern population of Raza was estimated at more than a million. In those days a few egg hunters sailing primitive dugout canoes voyaged from settlements along the gulf to gather gull and tern eggs. In a poor country every possible food is utilized. The egg hunters' methods were crude. First they destroyed all the eggs laid before their arrival, to be sure that all of the eggs they subsequently gathered were fresh. Then they collected thousands of these fresh eggs. The invaders departed, however, before the laying season was over, so that some of the birds produced young and the gulls and terns survived.

But by the early 1960s the egg hunters had stepped up their activities. Some 18 or 20 canoes propelled by outboard motors would arrive on Raza, and the hunters would stay throughout the laying season, collecting hundreds of thousands of eggs. As a result the breeding flocks of Heermann's gulls and elegant terns dwindled to a few thousand. The threatened extinction of these two species—the royal terns had breeding grounds elsewhere as well and were not dying out as a species —was brought to public attention largely through the efforts of the late Lewis Wayne Walker, associate director of the Arizona-Sonora Desert Museum in Tucson. Prodded by Walker, groups of naturalists and scientists, Mexican and American, persuaded the Mexican government in 1964 to declare Raza a bird sanctuary. Wardens were stationed on the island to turn back egg seekers. The flocks of gulls and terns, one of the most awesome of Baja California's natural wonders, began to come back. The breeding population of gulls has recently been estimated at as high as 100,000, of elegant terns at 200,000.

Man is not the only predator that disturbs the realm of the breeding

An annual scuffle for nesting space at Raza Island sanctuary pits white elegant terns against an encircling swarm of Heermann's gulls.

birds. Some of the islands in the Gulf of California support pairs of peregrine falcons—also called duck hawks. Superb hunters, they are among the handsomest of predatory birds. They have extraordinary vision that enables them to change focus from nearby objects to those far away much the way a zoom lens does. With their great flying speed and murderous talons, peregrines have no difficulty catching their prey —ducks, murrelets, petrels, even some of the smaller gulls—nailing their victims in mid-air or driving them to earth. A falcon aerie can usually be spotted by the mound of clean-picked bones on the ground beneath it. Fierce as they are, peregrines are excellent parents. When their three or four red, almost spherical eggs hatch, the parent birds lavish food and care on their young. But they have a strong sense of territoriality, driving away other predatory birds, including their own kind. When the young peregrines mature they leave the parental nest and are forced to find a territory of their own in an area unoccupied by other peregrines.

But the peregrines, never numerous, are becoming rare. They are susceptible to the eggshell-softening effect of pesticide pollution. It has been estimated that two thirds of all the DDT ever produced is still in existence. Most of it, sooner or later, drains into the sea where it is absorbed by fish and other marine organisms that are eaten by birds, which, in turn, may be eaten by other birds such as the falcon. The eggs that afflicted birds lay have shells so thin that they may collapse of their own weight, to say nothing of the weight of the nesting bird.

Among other Baja-dwelling victims of DDT are ospreys and bald eagles, once frequently seen on the peninsula, as well as the commoner cormorants and brown pelicans. The visitor cruising among the islands or loafing on the beach at Bahía de los Angeles may find it hard to imagine that the pelicans are a threatened species. Here they are abundant —and a delight to the viewer, living proof that awkwardness need not be a handicap. Pelicans are large birds, and their movements are for the most part ponderous and clumsy. On land they tend to waddle, but they do it sedately, chin on chest. They maintain the same position when floating on water—until a fish comes by. Then the neck straightens out like an uncoiled spring. The immense bill seizes the fish, raises it in the air and turns it so that it is pointed headfirst toward the pelican's throat. Of all birds, the pelican is the greatest conformist. If one yawns to air its great throat pouch, all nearby pelicans yawn. If one stretches its wings to the full span of six feet, its neighbors stretch their wings. Flying in stately formation over bay or sea, they carefully maintain the same rhythm of flight—flap-flap-glide, flap-flap-flap-glide —like a well-drilled but overweight chorus line.

The pelican is an ancient bird, a prominent citizen of the warm seas of the world since pre-Miocene times, 30 million years ago. Now it appears to be doomed. In the past few decades it has disappeared from the gulf coast of the southern United States. More recently pelicans have begun to disappear from Alta California's coastal islands; the apparent cause in this instance is the pesticide content of the Pacific Ocean. The blight has spread to the islands along the Pacific coast of Baja California. Worthless soft-shelled pelican eggs have been found in nests as far south as the San Benito Islands, more than 300 miles below the Mexican-American border. Even in the Gulf of California, the apparently thriving state of the pelican population may be deceptive. A population collapse takes a long time to become apparent, particularly in a long-lived species. Pesticides are used in the huge drainage basin of the Colorado River that feeds into the gulf and the threat of pollution—and extinction—is there.

Who needs pelicans? Nobody, perhaps, except those of us who like to sit on lonely beaches and watch birds. But there is a grim omen in what is happening to the pelican. Because it is big, awkward, funny and conspicuous, its disappearance, if and when it occurs, will be easily noticed. What of the less obvious forms of sea life—the smaller, more elusive birds? What about the fish in the sea? It was not long ago that optimists talked of the sea as a safeguard against famine in an over-crowded world. Fishermen here on the gulf complain that fishing is not what it used to be—but this is a chronic fisherman's complaint everywhere, seldom taken seriously. Sitting in the sand at Bahía de los Angeles, however, remembering some gloomy words of Joseph Jehl of the San Diego Natural History Museum, you consider the pelican's prospects with utmost seriousness. "Unless man learns," Dr. Jehl said, "to view these declining species as indicators of the extent to which the ecosystem is infected . . . the 30-million-year life span of the pelican clan will exceed that of *Homo sapiens* by a wide margin."

Teeming Life on a Barren Rock

PHOTOGRAPHS BY JOHN BLAUSTEIN

San Pedro Mártir is a sun-baked rock pile jutting up from the middle of the Gulf of California 30 miles west of Baja. It is less than a square mile in area, with sheer, 1,000-foot cliffs of lava and sandstone. Swept by dry winds, watered by less than three inches of rain a year, the island gives an impression of barrenness that is further emphasized by the cardon cacti bristling along its summit.

Yet San Pedro Mártir is very much alive. Thousands of sea birds—boobies, pelicans, gulls and tropic birds —congregate on every available inch of rock ledge and pebble-strewn soil. Hundreds of sea lions cluster along its broken shoreline. Rattlesnakes and exotic lizards slither among the stones and cactus.

In its abundant wildlife, San Pedro is typical of the gulf's many scattered islands. The reason for the crowded animal populations of these almost plantless places is the wealth of the surrounding waters. Surging up and down the narrow gulf, tidal currents stir up nutrients from the depths and agitate the water so that unusually large amounts of oxygen are absorbed at the surface. In this fruitful environment, the minuscule marine organisms called plankton thrive in myriads; fish flourish on the plankton, and sea birds and sea lions feast on the fish.

Among the birds of San Pedro that enjoy this ample harvest, the most numerous are the blue-footed and brown boobies. On land, where they sleep, lay their eggs (*right*) and rear their young, the boobies cut awkward, comical figures that justify the name bestowed on them by early mariners. But at sea they belie their name by the deft grace with which they dive and plunge beneath the surface in their search for fish.

San Pedro's animal inhabitants also include species that are neither feathered nor finny—such as the common rat, introduced by the boats of guano collectors from the mainland, and the diamondback rattler, similar to that found in the western United States and Mexico.

Two varieties of lizard are unique to this tiny place: the spotted and stubby *Uta palmeri,* and its longer, slimmer relative, known only by its jaw-breaking Latin name of *Cnemidophorus tigris martyris.* Although only a scientist's eye could tell these reptiles apart from mainland lizards, the minute differences they have acquired during eons of the island's isolation are enough to classify them as San Pedro's own.

Two blue-footed boobies incubate their eggs on the rocky soil of San Pedro Mártir. The rugged island, whitened by the guano of generations of sea birds, abounds with cardon cacti, but contains little other vegetation.

A BROWN PELICAN IN FLIGHT

SEA LIONS SPORTING OFFSHORE

A SALLY LIGHTFOOT CRAB AT HOME

FRIENDLY NEIGHBORS: SEA LIONS, PELICANS AND HEERMANN'S GULLS

A COLONY OF SEA ANEMONES

A WESTERN DIAMONDBACK RATTLER

A PELICAN NESTING AMONG CARDON CACTI

INSECT-EATING LIZARDS AND FISH-EATING PELICAN CHICKS

A TROPIC BIRD ALOFT

RED-BILLED TROPIC BIRDS NESTING IN ROCKS

SAN PEDRO'S OWN LIZARD, UTA PALMERI

BLUE-FOOTED BOOBY CHICKS, STILL FLUFFY WITH DOWN

BROWN PELICAN CHICKS IN A NEST OF TWIGS

A BROWN BOOBY STANDING ITS GROUND

A BLUE-FOOTED BOOBY PAIR, THE MALE IDENTIFIABLE BY SMALLER PUPILS

6/ Pacific Lagoons and Islands

Some of these lagoons extended twenty miles inland....Here in these secluded nooks, whales taught their newly born calves to swim.

WALTER NORDHOFF/ *THE JOURNEY OF THE FLAME*

Baja California is one of the corners of the world in which a few animals appear to be holding their own—or even gaining a little—in their battle to survive man's destructiveness. In the bays, lagoons and offshore islands of Baja's Pacific coast at least three marine mammals that were thought to be headed for extinction—the gray whale, the Guadalupe fur seal and the elephant seal—have managed to reestablish themselves. Their survival is both an ecological miracle and an eloquent tribute to the virtues of Baja's isolation.

The most spectacular of the three mammals is the gray whale. Once killed in wholesale numbers, the gray was believed doomed a half century ago. But now each year, from late December through March, the lagoons of Baja's west coast swarm with about 10,000 of these great creatures, courting, breeding and giving birth to their young. Their recovery is due in part to international protective agreements, reinforced by enlightened conservation measures taken by the Mexican government. But no protective measures could have saved the gray whale had it not been for the peculiar nature of the bays, lagoons and inlets that notch this lonely coast.

Three bay-and-lagoon complexes lure the grays to Baja's Pacific coast. The most southerly is Bahía Magdalena; because it is near the tropics, its many lagoons are bordered with mangrove swamps. Some 175 miles to the north is Bahía de Ballenas (Whales Bay), with the 20-

mile-long Laguna San Ignacio emptying into it. Some 120 miles still farther to the northwest lies Punta Eugenia, a fishhook of rocky land extending westward into the Pacific; this point of land partially encloses the largest of Baja's bays, Bahía Sebastián Vizcaíno, named for the Spanish mariner Sebastián Vizcaíno, who explored this coast in 1602. Three lagoons open into Bahía Sebastián Vizcaíno: Manuela on the north, Guerrero Negro (Black Warrior) in the center and, in the bottom of the fishhook, the largest lagoon of all. Mexicans know it as Laguna Ojo de Liebre, or Jack Rabbit Springs Lagoon (for an old waterhole located near the lagoon's eastern end). Americans usually refer to it as Scammon's Lagoon after a Yankee whaling captain who played a melancholy role in the lagoon's natural history.

The land bordering these three lagoons is picturesque, but quite inhospitable to man—all dunes and sandy plains, with little vegetation. There are a few elephant trees and some stands of yucca and cactus, but most of the country is bare. The sand is soft and unstable, constantly moving with the wind. Pacific tides and storms have carved waterways far back into the desert. High tides frequently cover the flats; the intense sunlight causes rapid evaporation, creating great salt basins, some of which are commercially harvested. But aside from the salt company town at Guerrero Negro and a few camps of turtle fishermen, the region of the three lagoons is an exceedingly empty and quiet part of the world.

The salty waters of the lagoons are glassy calm—perfect places for female gray whales to have their calves. The ocean beyond is turbulent, breaking violently over the sandbars that parallel the shore and separate the lagoons from the sea. This uproar does not bother the grays that are mating—in fact, they appear to enjoy it. But the sandbars and churning waves make this a treacherous stretch of the Pacific coast for men and boats—shipwreck country. The wind-whipped dunes and beaches, particularly those on either side of the entrance to Ojo de Liebre, are a beachcomber's paradise—a great catch basin into which the prevailing northwest wind drives all manner of strange things: the wreckage of ships—timbers, hatch covers, rope; glass floats from fishing nets; barrels, buoys and bottles of every description, many of them turned lavender or purple by the intense light of the sun. Everything seems battered, faded, ancient. I have found myself wondering if some of these relics could have come from the 17th Century Spanish galleons that rounded Punta Eugenia on voyages of Pacific exploration and were never heard of again.

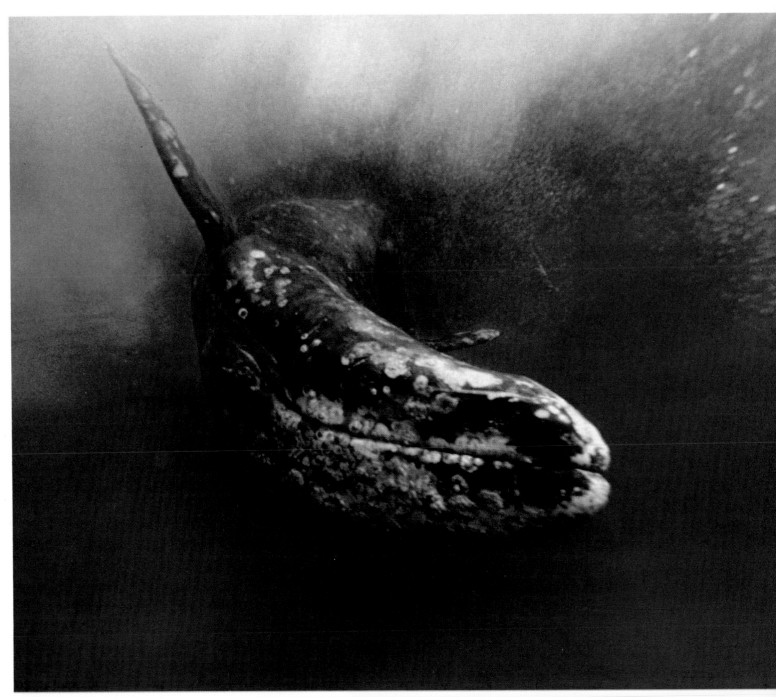

A barnacle-encrusted gray whale about to give birth thrashes in labor off the Pacific coast on her way south to the Baja calving grounds.

Not long ago I flew to Ojo de Liebre with my old friend Francisco Muñoz in his small plane. In mid-March we were not so much interested in beachcombing, which is good at any time of the year, as in seeing whales. March marks the end of the seasonal visitation of gray whales to these Pacific lagoons and we wanted to see them before they all took off on their yearly 5,000-mile migration to their summer pastures in the Bering Strait and other arctic waters off Alaska. Muñoz said that a month earlier the whales had been as "thick as sardines" in Ojo de Liebre; we hoped that at least some of them might still be there.

We flew much of the way down on the gulf side of the peninsula because of thick fogs that shroud Baja's Pacific coast in the spring months. Turning inland at Bahía San Luis Gonzaga, we climbed to cross the mountains. Far below I could see El Mármol, and with binoculars I could pick out the onyx schoolhouse where I had camped. We came out on the Pacific coast, fortunately now clear of fog, at the fishing camp of Santa Rosalillita and flew south over broad beaches. Since the tide was low, Muñoz said we would try landing on the beach just at the entrance to Ojo de Liebre. He lowered the plane gradually, and gently touched the sand with the wheels to test its firmness. Fortunately the sand was solid and we came to a safe stop a short distance from the mouth of the lagoon.

Immediately we could see the vapor plumes of spouting whales. After the first spout, the great mottled gray-and-black hulk of the whale's body would rise. There would be several more spouts. The body would curve slightly, showing the gray's characteristic ridge of knobs along the lower spine; then the creature would sink. Out in mid-channel, where deeper dives were possible, the whales threw their huge flukes, or tail fins, in the air before diving downward. A way off one whale repeatedly breached the water, hurling at least half of its huge body out, then falling back in with a tremendous splash. Most of the whales were in groups of two or three. Breeding was still going on in the seaward end of the lagoon—a favored mating area.

We stood on a sand dune and watched the grays for an hour or so. They were not "thick as sardines," as Muñoz said they had been in February, but they were still there in abundance. Later we flew low over the inland parts of the lagoon. From the plane we could see mother whales with calves—sleek and glossy infants, not yet scarred with barnacles. The water was as calm as a millpond, giving the calves the best chance of survival in their first few seconds of life, from their underwater birth to their first gasp of air at the surface. The old whalers

called this part of the lagoon the nursery; they might better have named it the slaughterhouse, because here in other years they had great success in killing both whale calves and their mothers.

Ojo de Liebre and other lagoons are the southern terminals of the gray whales' 10,000-mile yearly round trip to the Bering Strait—one of the strangest and most arduous of all animal migrations. The gray is a medium-sized whale, 35 to almost 50 feet in length and from 20 to 40 tons in weight; the females are slightly larger than the males. Although the animal's basic color is black, a mature one has a mottled gray appearance because of the number of barnacles that fasten themselves to its hide; if the barnacle dies and falls off, or is scraped off, a patch of white scar tissue becomes exposed.

All whales are descended from creatures that lived on land a hundred million years ago. In time these ancestors abandoned the land and returned to a marine habitat. Their front legs became flippers and they developed great horizontal flukes in their tails for propulsive power. But the whales continued to breathe air through a blowhole in the top of the head. They also continued to bring forth their young in a living state and to suckle them, as do all mammals.

Of all the whales, the gray maintained (or reacquired) the closest affinity for the land. Most of the great whales frequent the deeper parts of the ocean; the gray cruises the coastal shallows and for the most critical phases of its life cycle, breeding and calf bearing, it seeks out calm lagoons. It even tolerates water so shallow that it can rest on the bottom —a condition that causes other whales to panic and often kills them (stranded, they suffocate beneath their own immense weight).

The gray whale once existed in the Atlantic and the North and Baltic Seas, but it now survives only in the Pacific. Its northern range is in the cold food-rich waters between Alaska and Siberia. Here the long arctic summer days create an explosion of marine growth, including the small, bottom-living amphipods that are the gray whale's principal food. The whale fills its mouth with water by the ton, then expels the water with its tongue through its baleen, a sievelike screen of whalebone—a hard but flexible material once much in demand for products ranging from toothpicks to corset stays. Small organisms stick in the sieve and these nutrients are then ingested into a series of stomach cavities, at the rate of perhaps one ton of food each day.

Gray whales graze for four or five months in their rich sea pastures of the north, storing up blubber. Then, as the arctic days shorten and

Surfacing in Scammon's Lagoon on the western Baja coast a gray whale "blows"—exhales condensed vapor. The spout can reach 10 feet.

the ocean begins to freeze, the herd heads south on the annual migration from the Bering Strait to Baja California. The whales swim steadily at a speed of about four knots—although they can put on bursts of 10-knot speed. If the moon is full, they may swim around the clock; if the moon is dark, they may rest for a few hours at night; their buoyancy allows them to swim and float almost effortlessly. Apparently they do not pause to eat either en route or, in fact, during the entire seven- or eight-month period it takes them to cover 10,000 or more miles and go through the cycles of breeding or giving birth. Their timing is uncannily accurate. From year to year there is rarely more than five days' variation in the beginning or end of their migration or in the date of their passage past any point along the route.

The first gray whales to reach Baja's lagoons arrive there in late December. Most of the early arrivals are females impregnated during the previous year's trip south. The gestation period is approximately 12 months. Some of the females reach the lagoons not a minute too soon, and some do not make it in time, giving birth along the open Pacific coast —and young whales thus born are often casualties if the seas are rough and stormy.

But safely within a Baja lagoon the female whale can have her calf in comfort and safety. The high salinity of the water at the head of the lagoon increases the whales' buoyancy. The pregnant cow will usually go to the most inland part of the lagoon, in water depths of 12 to 48 feet. The newborn whale is usually from 14 to 17 feet long, and weighs between 1,500 and 3,000 pounds. The average is probably about one ton, compared with the mother's 35 tons or so—the equivalent of a 140-pound woman giving birth to a four-pound baby.

Like any newborn creature, the young whale is vulnerable; it must quickly get to the surface for air. The mother may help by prodding it upward with her head or she may submerge and rise again with the baby safely on her back. The mother nurses the infant from either of two recessed nipples at the rear of her underside. After the young whale has taken the nipple into its mouth, making a waterproof seal with its tongue and palate, it is ready to eat, but it does not suck. Instead, the mother, by contracting her abdominal muscles, shoots a jet of milk into the baby's throat, a gallon or so at a time. The milk is heavy and rich, about eight times as rich in fat as human milk, but without sugar. The baby gains weight rapidly. By the time the northward migration starts, after two months in the lagoon, the calf may have reached a length of 20 feet and weigh 4,500 to 5,000 pounds.

A gray whale breaches in Scammon's Lagoon. Some scientists believe that whales execute this maneuver—rising out of the depths, then splashing down —in order to scratch their barnacled and lice-infested backs; others believe breaching is simply playful. Old-time whalers saw it differently. The leaps, charges and thrashings of the "devil fish" represented violent danger to them in their fragile whaling boats.

The young whales are normally the only ones that appear sleek and well fed on the northward journey. The adults, having eaten little or nothing since the previous summer, are gaunt and move more slowly than they did on the trip south. The mothers have been further reduced by giving birth and by nursing. They nevertheless continue to nurse their young throughout the trip north, the calf swimming at its mother's side, learning about the migratory route that it will follow for the rest of its life. It is weaned at the age of six months in the summer abundance of the northern seas and by autumn is large and strong enough to make the trip unaided with the rest of the herd to its birthplace in Baja.

While the pregnant females are bearing and nursing their calves far back in Baja's lagoons, the other whales are vigorously courting and breeding. Some of these activities take place in the open ocean, some outside the lagoon where the surf breaks over the sandbars, some in the lagoon itself. Since the females are in season only every other year and the herd is more or less equally divided between the sexes, each mating female is usually attended by at least two males. There appears to be no violence to the rivalry among the males. The unsuccessful ones merely turn away and search elsewhere or may even hang around as spectators. Both courting and mating are accompanied by much thrashing and rolling. John Barrymore, whose film credits included the part of Captain Ahab in *Moby Dick,* witnessed one of these Brobdingnagian unions while cruising Baja waters. Barrymore wrote of his awe at the sight of this "amorous dalliance . . . if anything so enviably and titanically active comes under the head of dalliance!"

The gray whale's gregariousness, its preference for coastal shallows and its high degree of visibility almost led to its extinction. Indians along the Canadian coast, using canoes and spears, had killed gray whales from time immemorial, but the death toll was slight in comparison with the size of the herd. And once the whales reached Baja's lonely lagoons they were unmolested—until the mid-19th Century.

At that time several shore whaling stations were established along the grays' migration route down the Alta California coast, and whaling ships began chasing grays in Baja's lagoons. Such hunting was called mudhole whaling, and it was not the most profitable branch of the industry. The gray yielded a grade of whale oil much less valuable than the premium waxy oil from sperm whales. And its baleen was of low quality for whalebone. There was a more immediate disadvantage from the whalers' point of view. Normally a peaceful, shy creature, the gray

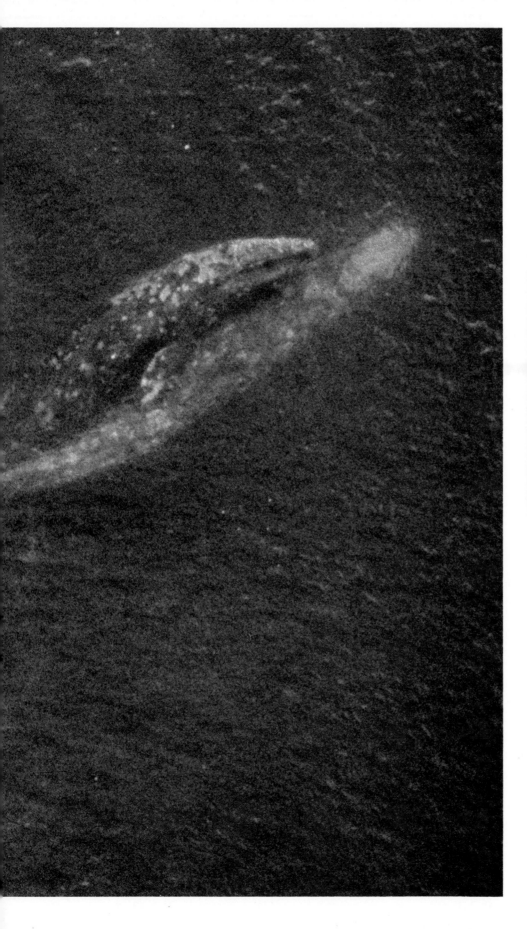

Male and female gray whales churn
the water (left) as they begin to mate
in Scammon's Lagoon. After mating
these huge mammals migrate
northward in the spring to their Arctic
feeding grounds. The following winter
they return to Baja where the females
bear their young in shallow inlets
and lagoons such as this. For half a
year mother and calf (above) are
inseparable. Over the winter the calf
nurses until it more than doubles its
one-ton birth weight. By spring it is
ready to follow the mother north and
learn to take the 10,000-mile round-
trip migration route on its own.

whale could, when molested, wounded or robbed of its young, become stupendously violent, butting whaleboats with its head or smashing them to splinters with its flukes. Sailors on whaling vessels called grays "devilfish" and one old whaler described the breed as "part sea serpent, part alligator."

In 1857, however, the wily Yankee skipper Charles Melville Scammon discovered a safe way to hunt grays. He had done some mudhole whaling in Bahía Magdalena the previous winter, and had run into bad luck. Two of his whaleboats had been destroyed by angry grays and his crew nursed an assortment of broken legs, arms, ribs and internal injuries. But in 1857 his brig, *Boston,* was light and his crew, having had a year to recover from their injuries, thirsted for action. Scammon decided to explore a large lagoon he had heard of that branched inland from Bahía Sebastián Vizcaíno, an area no whaler had investigated. Passage into the lagoon—over a sandbar and through a heavy swell—was difficult, but once inside, Scammon was rewarded with the sight of gray whales in unbelievable numbers in the lagoon's serene, almost landlocked waters. Trying to harpoon them in the conventional way, though, was disastrous. Boats were lost and men injured. But Scammon had an idea. He armed his men with bomb lances—harpoons with explosive gunpowder charges in their heads—and instructed them to moor their whaleboats near the shore in water so shallow that the whales could not approach close enough to smash them. The men were, in effect, bombing whales from the desert shores of Ojo de Liebre—and the technique worked. By the end of the two-month season Scammon's men had killed so many whales that every receptacle aboard the *Boston* was being used to store oil.

News of Scammon's whale bonanza got around. By the seasons of 1858 and 1859 scores of large whaling vessels were at work along the Baja coast. Where once the only sound had been the spouting of the whales and the splash of their breaching, there was now a bedlam of rattling ship's gear and detonating harpoon bombs. Scammon later estimated that between 1846, when the first mudholing had begun, and 1874, 10,000 gray whales were killed. The slaughter resumed in the 20th Century. Modern whaling methods, using not only explosive harpoons but powerboats and factory ships, made for an even rapider form of slaughter. The gray whale herd, which had once numbered about 25,000, was down to some 250 and a great mammal seemed on its way to extinction.

Finally, however, international agreements were signed in 1937 and

1946 that forbade the killing of gray whales. The mottled leviathans began to come back. Their migratory destinations have changed somewhat over the years. A century ago hundreds of them stopped in San Diego Bay in Alta California, but urbanization and sea traffic discouraged them. The large numbers that once wintered in Baja's Bahía Magdalena and its lagoons have also diminished. There is heavy boat traffic there, and increasing agricultural development of the surrounding land. Sizable numbers of whales were found at one time in Laguna de Guerrero Negro, just to the north of Ojo de Liebre, but the development of the salt industry and considerable boat traffic have driven many of them away. However, some of the whales have sought the quiet and isolation of Laguna San Ignacio, farther to the south, and the Mexican government has recently declared Ojo de Liebre an "aquatic refuge" for whales.

Meanwhile the whale migration has become a prime attraction for coastal watchers from San Francisco south. Each year during the winter months people gather by the thousands at Point Loma in San Diego to watch the stately procession of spouts at sea. Or they board charter boats to cruise slowly along the migratory paths, counting spouts, staring with awe as the huge barnacle-covered hulks rise to the surface. For those who want to follow the migration, such organizations as the San Diego Natural History Museum arrange week-long charters. In this way really dedicated whale watchers have joined the whales in Ojo de Liebre, where the trippers have boarded small boats and gotten almost within touching distance.

A research associate at the San Diego Natural History Museum and a veteran of the U.S. Fish and Wildlife Service, Raymond M. Gilmore, has been studying the gray whale since 1952. He observes that it is more valuable alive than it ever was when being reduced to oil on the deck of a 19th Century whaling ship, more valuable than it would be today being converted into food for cats and dogs. Alive, it provides cultural and esthetic enrichment as well as hard cash from tourism—a possible future source of revenue for the poor and isolated Pacific coast of Baja California. It also functions as a living laboratory for scientific investigations. Cardiologists are interested in studying this warm-blooded creature's heart. Oceanographers and researchers in underwater communications have studied the sounds the whales make, which are apparently a subtle combination of conversation and sonar.

Gilmore notes also that with the recovery of the gray whale herd there will be increasing pressure for resumption of commercial whaling. "The forces of conservation will meet the forces of exploitation head-on," he predicts. "Let us hope that understanding prevails. If limited and tightly regulated commercial killing of gray whales is permitted, it must be balanced by a deep and genuine concern for preservation of the species with inspection of operations and a quota on the harvest. The gray whale has only recently come back from the brink of oblivion."

The remarkable recovery of the gray whale in Baja California has been duplicated by other species. One of them, the Guadalupe fur seal, was believed to be entirely extinct. Because of its luxuriant fur this long-nosed, big-flippered seal had been killed off in wholesale fashion since early in the 19th Century—and by mid-century was thought to have disappeared as a species. But in 1926 two fishermen discovered a small herd of about 60 of these seals surviving on Guadalupe Island and captured two of them. One of the fishermen, William Clover, sold this pair to the San Diego Zoo. Then, for reasons unknown, he quarreled with the zoo director, returned to Guadalupe and spitefully killed as many of the rest of the herd as he could find. He took the skins to Panama for sale and died there in a barroom fight. But Clover's malicious act did not, fortunately, do in the fur seal for good. In 1954, after a long search, Carl Hubbs of the Scripps Institution of Oceanography finally discovered 14 of the supposedly extinct animals on an isolated rocky shore of Guadalupe Island. Subsequent expeditions disclosed more, and the present population is thought to be approximately 500—which is perhaps 1/1,000 of the number that once lived in these waters. Still, a population of 500 is better than none at all, and the Guadalupe fur seal now promises to survive as a species.

The third and most grotesque mammal to escape extinction by virtue of Baja's isolation is the northern elephant seal, or sea elephant, the largest and strangest member of the pinniped, or "fin foot," family. Full-grown males reach overall lengths of 16 feet or more and weigh one to two tons. The females are much smaller—8 to 10 feet long and half a ton or so in weight—and they lack the most distinctive feature of the species: a large and flexible proboscis that looks like a bobbed and malformed elephant's trunk. Warning rivals away from his harem during the December-to-February breeding season, the male elephant seal puts the end of the trunk in his mouth and blows, producing a blend of a snort and a roar. If the challenger chooses to fight, the male has to get

Rare fur seals bask on the lonely rocks of Guadalupe Island, the last refuge of the species in its fight against extinction.

his trunk out of the way to expose his teeth. And fight they do; many of the males are deeply scarred from waterfront battles. The contest resolved, the victor may return to the cows or may simply collapse on the shore. His slow-paced deep breathing resonates in the trunk, resulting in what is probably the world's most resounding snore. Young bulls that have not yet reached the breeding and fighting stage have been known to test their developing trunks by swimming into a sea cave, blowing into their trunks and using the cave as an echo chamber.

The elephant seal is a powerful swimmer and deep diver. Approached at sea it will often raise itself vertically in the water, stare calmly at any intruder, then sink slowly from sight. But ashore the seal has difficulty maneuvering its bulk. Its hind flippers are virtually useless on land; fore flippers offer little support for the great body. The animal moves itself by undulation, the fat body quivering like jelly. Breeding is indiscriminate and awkward. Newborn seals are frequently victims of their elders' monumental clumsiness, being either crushed or suffocated under the weight of the older seals. The young that survive all this hurly-burly, however, grow rapidly in size and strength. They double their 50- to 70-pound birth weight within a few weeks. The elephant seal's milk, like that of the whale, is prodigiously rich in fat.

Like the whale, too, the elephant seal stores up quantities of fat or blubber that can be melted down for oil. For this reason elephant seals were hunted and killed by the same men who hunted whales—only the killing was considerably easier. Elephant seals are lethargic and amazingly unafraid of men—and on land, unable to do much about fleeing even if afraid. Captain Scammon, the man who opened up the rich whaling grounds of Ojo de Liebre, was also an elephant seal hunter.

Cedros, the San Benitos and Guadalupe, all islands off Baja's Pacific coast, were among Scammon's most productive elephant seal grounds. As he described the hunt: "The sailors get between the herd and the water; then, raising all possible noise . . . the party advances slowly toward the rookery. . . . Occasionally an overgrown male will give battle, or attempt to escape; but a musket ball through the brain dispatches it; or someone checks its progress by thrusting a lance into the roof of its mouth, which causes it to settle on its haunches, when two men with heavy, oaken clubs give the creature repeated blows about the head, until it is stunned or killed. . . . The onslaught creates such a panic among these peculiar creatures that, losing all control of their actions, they climb, roll and tumble over each other. . . . In one instance where 65 were captured, several were found showing no signs of having been either clubbed or lanced, but were smothered by numbers of their kind heaped upon them. The whole flock, when attacked, manifested alarm by their peculiar roar, the sound of which, among the largest males, is nearly as loud as the lowing of an ox, but more prolonged."

Captain Scammon added a sad afterthought: "Owing to the continual pursuit of the animals, they have become nearly if not quite extinct on the California coast, or the remaining few have fled to some unknown point for security."

The hunting of elephant seals began in the early 1800s and ranged north from Baja California to Point Reyes near San Francisco. By the 1880s the seals had become rare, and by 1892 Guadalupe Island was their only known remaining refuge. In that year eight elephant seals were seen on the island and seven were killed; extinction of the species seemed complete. Twenty years later, however, a herd of 125 was discovered on Guadalupe Island at a place now called Elephant Beach, and the herd continued to grow. In 1922 President Alvaro Obregón of Mexico, prompted by the urging of the California Academy of Sciences and other institutions, declared the island a wildlife reservation and prohibited the killing of seals. The elephant seal quickly benefited from this action. The herd continued to grow, establishing rookeries on other islands and extending its range up the Alta California coast.

It is questionable whether the elephant seal, the Guadalupe fur seal or the great gray whale could have made it anywhere but in almost unpopulated, isolated Baja California and on its offshore islands. That they have survived even there is something of a miracle. And this, perhaps, is one of the greatest wonders of Baja, that a region so seemingly dead and sterile is, in fact, an abundant giver and protector of life.

A Seal Saved from Extinction

One hundred and fifty miles off the Pacific coast of Baja California lies Guadalupe, an isolated volcanic island that towers 4,000 feet above the ocean's surface. The island is a formidable place to approach. Its eroded lava shores are indented with a few small coves rimmed by narrow, sandy beaches, but there are no harbors. The depth of the water close to shore makes it difficult for vessels to anchor and the Pacific swells hinder the landing of boats.

In the 19th Century, men surmounted these obstacles in pursuit of a valuable prize: the oil of the northern elephant seal, which with its cousin in the Southern Hemisphere is the largest seal on earth. For several months each year these mammals swarm to the Guadalupe beaches to breed and bear their young. Terribly vulnerable on land, the elephant seals were systematically slaughtered until, by 1900, they were believed to be all but extinct.

Providentially a few survived, protected by Guadalupe's most inaccessible beaches and, later, by decree of the Mexican government. Gradually the seals have multiplied from the 125 animals counted by a visitor to Guadalupe in 1911 to an estimated 15,000 today. The revitalized species has outgrown its Guadalupe refuge; herds now crowd the shores of many other west coast islands.

It is not surprising that the elephant seals, given half a chance, should have bounced back so rapidly. Every mature female of the species spends virtually all her life pregnant. The gestation period is almost exactly one year. Pregnant cows come ashore in late December, usually just in time to bear their pups, and shortly after the bulls have staked out territories on the beach. Within weeks the cows, now in the harems of the strongest bulls, are pregnant again; their female pups will be mothers themselves within three years. And so the herds increase geometrically.

But there are natural population controls. Some pups die of disease, some drown before they learn to swim and others are taken by sharks when the herds return to the sea. Other pups never even survive that long; they fall victim to their elders' ponderous proceedings across the beach. While the cows show some concern for the young, the bulls do not, and every year after the herd leaves, the beach is littered with the carcasses of young seals crushed by their heedless sires.

A docile female elephant seal reposes trustingly on a Guadalupe Island beach. Whiskers are characteristic of both sexes of elephant seals, but the female lacks the appendage that gives the species its name—the prominent trunklike proboscis sported by the bull.

In full fighting trim, a dominant bull, or harem master (left), threatens mayhem to an intruder approaching his domain. When a rival bull nears, a harem master rears up, elevates his trunk, lowers it into his mouth and, using mouth and throat as an echo chamber, emits a resonant bong that often succeeds in frightening off the enemy.

Two enraged bulls, harem master and intruder, clash in shallow water near the beach after the trespasser ignored the other's threatening roar. Butting heavily and using two-inch canine teeth to gouge each other, the bulls are bruised and bloodied in such engagements, but the battles are usually short and seldom fought to the death. The loser breaks off and slinks away to the outskirts of the harem.

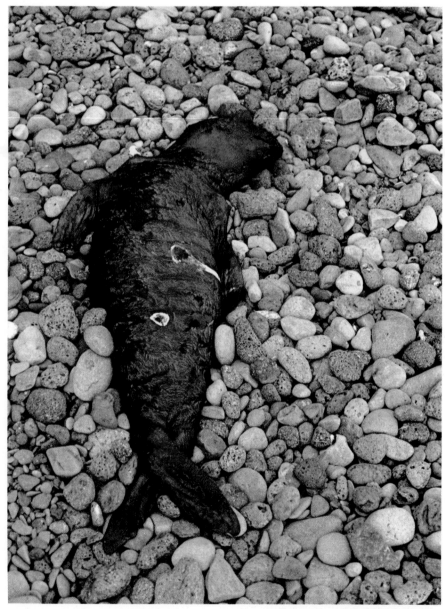

An elephant seal herd (left) dozes
below the cliffs of Guadalupe. Between
frenzies of fighting and mating, the
seals often drowse, moving only to flip
a covering of sand over themselves.

One of many casualties of the breeding
season, a pup lies dead on the beach,
victim of a two-ton bull's passage. Most
pups survive, though, and go to
sea when two to three months old.

A mature bull quietly suns his scarred, bulbous trunk and hind flippers.

A bewhiskered yearling elephant seal snoozes muzzle up in placid water.

Surrounded by a swarm of tiny seagoing crabs, a bull wallows offshore. The crabs have little to fear—elephant seals prefer squid and fish.

7/ The Southern Reaches

*All the other and very varied attempts to
"develop" the area ... have ended in dismal failure, for the
land has always returned to its own wild self.*

JOSEPH WOOD KRUTCH/ *THE FORGOTTEN PENINSULA*

Coming south from Scammon's Lagoon past the mid-point of the Baja
Peninsula the road is long, rough and monotonous. On the right are the
vast and dreary stretches of the Vizcaíno Desert, known in one part as
the Llano Perdido (Lost Plain) and in another as the Llano del Berrendo
(Antelope Plain—although I saw no antelope or any other kind of life).
The track is alternately deep sand and broken rock. On the left there is
an uninviting tangle of jagged peaks. Then, finally, you crest a hill and
your eye follows the descending road to a glittering green-blue gem in
the desert. This is a spring-fed oasis, bordered by thick stands of stately date palms planted after the Jesuit fathers had established the
mission of San Ignacio here in 1728. Wherever gravity takes the spring
water there is lush vegetation—grapes, figs, pomegranates, grains, sugar cane, vegetables and flowers. The town of San Ignacio, which has
grown up around this life-giving water and the bounty it produces, is
one of the simplest and most peaceful places on the peninsula. The
houses cluster around the old mission church and a laurel-shaded pla-
za. The pace of life is slow, easy, untouched by tourism and totally un-
affected by the bustle of the 20th Century.

At the edge of town, where the spring water does not flow, the earth
is again inhospitable, bare, seemingly sterile and littered with volcanic
rock. The source of some of this rock is apparent on the northeastern horizon—three peaks known as Las Tres Vírgenes, The Three Virgins. No

one seems to know the reason for the name, which suggests delicacy and gentleness. But these peaks are dark and menacing and are thought to be the most recently active volcanoes on the peninsula. In their foothills lies one of the most formidable of the peninsula's mountain passes. It is appropriately known as Cuesta del Infiernillo, or Little Hell Hill. Through it you work your way down to the gulf coast plain.

I found myself on a blacktop road again and enjoying it—with a twinge of guilt, like a reformed drinker taking the first step off the wagon. I thought of a remark Joseph Wood Krutch made in his loving book about Baja, *The Forgotten Peninsula:* Baja is a "splendid example of how much bad roads can do for a country." Wilderness areas survive best in a condition of inaccessibility—or, better yet, of impenetrability. This is true of all wilderness areas, but particularly so of a desert wilderness. A desert is a fragile place. Its vegetation and wildlife endure only through the most precarious sort of balance. Tamper with that balance and you may destroy it forever. Damage a plant even slightly and you may break its tenuous hold on life. Move a stone and you may dislocate the life of a desert creature. It is easy to mar the beauty of the landscape; tire tracks and footprints can leave permanent scars. Even in the most primitive sections of the peninsula, I had seen discouraging evidence of man's intrusion: rocks daubed with graffiti or with paint to mark the route for off-road car races, discarded clothing, blown tires, broken fan belts and everywhere the litter of cans that once contained motor oil, beans, sardines or beer.

But, while I agree philosophically with Krutch about the relationship of bad roads to wilderness, such an aphorism would be lost on the people who call this country home. Even in the most rugged parts of the peninsula local residents spontaneously volunteer their labor to keep the crude roads in shape. A road is their only connection with the world, and for them a better road is a better connection—a way to schools, medical services, supplies, a market for their goods.

And so I had mixed feelings as I cruised down the new highway south along the gulf coast. Places that 10 years before I had struggled to reach were now easily accessible. The strings of loaded burros and the laboring old trucks loaded with gasoline tins or with entire families were now replaced by big, modern trucks, nimble pickups and private cars. The little palm-bordered river at Mulegé was as refreshing as ever, although the village's pace was not quite so leisurely as it once had been. Bahía Concepción, a 25-mile-long bay running south from Mulegé, was still lovely. Nothing short of a cataclysm could alter it—a blue and placid little sea, shut off from the gulf by a sandy, mountainous point of land, Punta Concepción. But the new highway runs close beside the bay and it has destroyed some of the magic. El Coyote, a cove that once gave the feeling of total detachment from the world, is now much visited, much littered; the tiny oysters and succulent lobsters that were once easily gathered here are greatly reduced in number.

Driving on south, I went past the town of Loreto and headed for Puerto Escondido, hoping it might have escaped this wave of change. Ten years before, it had been exactly what its name means, a hidden port. There are two bays, a larger one on the outside shielded from the open gulf by a cluster of islands, and a tiny inner cove, almost landlocked, connected with the outer bay by a channel no wider than a stone's throw. Once Puerto Escondido was little known, seldom seen, and one of the most enchanting places on the peninsula. The water was full of fish, the shores crowded with birds, all in a jewellike setting with the island-dotted gulf on one side and pastel mountains on the other.

Now, I discovered, the new highway runs close to the shore. More, the Mexican government has built a steel and concrete pier jutting into the outer bay. There were campers on the beach and a large yacht moored in the inner bay. The sense of isolation was, sadly, gone. But the beauty of the place was almost unimpaired. Birds were still there in great numbers as were fish. In fact, the new pier provides an excellent observation platform for watching the schools of bait, mullet and sierra mackerel—and the occasional dark shadow of a larger fish—in the deep, clear water. As I left, a kit fox trotted across the path in front of me, apparently as much at home here as it had ever been.

South of Puerto Escondido, the road turns southwest into the steep grades of the Sierra Giganta. I noticed that the vegetation was showing subtle changes. The greens were greener here than they had been farther north, and the flowers more brilliant, particularly a rich yellow morning glory and a vine that laces the desert scrub and produces a brilliant crimson flower, known locally as *flor de San Miguel,* or St. Michael's flower. The cardons here grow in thick groves, called *cardonales.* These cacti are smaller, less monumental than those of the central desert, perhaps because they are crowded so close together.

The watershed on the gulf side is short and abrupt, with great cliffs and plunging canyons, as it is in most of the mountain ranges to the north. But the western face of the Sierra Giganta is long and sloping, leveling out into the broad Magdalena Plain, an area that is being intensively farmed, in many places with irrigation from wells. It was apparent that there had been a recent rain—this was early October. Broad, shallow sandy stream beds were running with rust-red water, and in some of the farming communities women and children stood and stared at this unaccustomed sight.

I knew that if there had been this much rain here, more had probably fallen to the south, bringing spectacular wild flowers. I hurried on to the cape region, at the very tip of the peninsula. While it is often as arid as the rest of the peninsula, this part of Baja usually catches the full brunt of the *chubascos*, storms that hit in the summer and early fall. When they do they may cause awesome destruction, but there is compensation in the floral explosion that usually follows.

I stopped in La Paz, southern Baja's territorial capital, long enough to pick up my wife, who had flown down to meet me. Then we headed toward Cabo San Lucas. Since my last visit a highway had been built all the way to this southernmost settlement of Baja. A trip that had once taken two days of uncomfortable travel could now be made in a matter of four hours or so by car. But we took it much more slowly, following side roads back into the hills or down to the beaches wherever possible. We rented a palm-thatched beach cottage at Bahía de las Palmas, a village 70 miles from Cabo San Lucas, as a base of operations. The cottage faced east, out across the lower end of the Gulf of California, and on the day we moved in, a thunderstorm threatened with heavy clouds and much lightning.

It was evident the next day that this country of the south had been well soaked by rains. There were still puddles of water in the stream beds, and the thickets of thorny scrub were ablaze with color. There were the same red *flores de San Miguel* and yellow morning-glories that I had seen farther north, but many more. The white-trunked *palo blanco*, a graceful tree found mainly in the southern half of Baja, appeared to be freshly washed, its leaves a brilliant green. There was *jícama*, a woody vine with rich red trumpet-shaped flowers giving off a heavy fragrance—a truly tropical smell. We saw at least two kinds of mallow, in different shades of orange, and a wild cotton plant, its large open yellow flowers decorated with splashes of red in their centers. Although it was early fall, the flowers were blooming as they do elsewhere in early summer. The last time I had been here the country was dry and brown, without a blossom in sight.

In the cape region the mountains, the highest on the peninsula south of the Sierra de Juárez and Sierra de San Pedro Mártir, are arranged differently from those in the rest of Baja; here the steep, abrupt slopes are on the Pacific side, while toward the gulf the mountains level out into rolling hills and plains. The mountains, too, showed signs of the rain. The pine and oak forests in the cloud-shrouded Sierra de la Laguna were a deep, rich green. The broad south-facing beaches—probably the most beautiful of the peninsula—were brilliantly white and unmarked; no one had walked on them since the storm, and the surf was still high. Resorts, some very luxurious, have begun to spring up along this coast, and one day it may be the Riviera of the New World. But for the present it is still largely empty and beautiful. It is not as empty as it was 10 years ago; still, we felt that we had it almost to ourselves except for gulls, pelicans, vultures and handsome caracaras—Mexican hawks that are both hunters and carrion eaters.

Cabo San Lucas is land's end. Here the peninsula disappears into the sea in a procession of huge, grotesquely eroded and tunneled boulders. The great swells from the Pacific surge around them, meeting the calmer, warmer water of the gulf. The sea here is rich in oxygen and nutrients and these attract fish of many sorts, including such game fish as marlin and sailfish. Cabo San Lucas has long been a commercial fishing center; the fishing boats and a tuna cannery provide employment for most of the inhabitants. Recently three resort hotels have been built nearby, all oriented toward sport fishing.

On this day, however, with the wind strong and the sea high, there were no fishing boats in sight as we climbed out on the rocks. In the lee of this rocky point Spanish galleons from Manila, loaded with silks and spices, once anchored to take on water after the long Pacific crossing. And here they were occasionally preyed upon by English privateers. Thomas Cavendish seized the galleon *Santa Ana* off this rocky point in 1587. Another rich haul was made in 1709 by the privateer Woodes Rogers. Capture of the galleon *Nuestra Señora de la Encarnación y Desengaño* made Rogers a wealthy man, but he could not say much for the country: " . . . full of mountains, unproductive. . . . Of all the places we have touched it is the least capable of supporting its inhabitants." A great place for larceny but no place to live.

An equally dim view of the cape was taken by János Xántus, a Hungarian naturalist who was stationed here from 1859 to 1861 as a tide observer for the United States Coast Survey. On the side he collected specimens of the local flora and fauna for Washington's Smithsonian Institution. In a letter to Spencer Baird of the Smithsonian, Xántus complained that he was "of God's grace nearly two years perched on this sandbeach, a laughingstock probably to the Pelicans and Turkey buzzards, the only signs of life around me. To the E and SE the eternally smoky Gulf, to all other points of the compass the sandy desert .... There is not a blade of grass in the country and not a green leaf."

Xántus was not quite as disenchanted as his letter would indicate. In Cabo San Lucas today he is given credit for the fact that some residents have fair skins and light eyes. He was also indefatigable as a specimen collector. By his own count, he sent the Smithsonian 92,000 plants, crustaceans, mollusks, mammals and so on. Some 3,825 of them, he claimed, were previously unknown species. These figures were probably inflated, but biologists today attribute many genuine discoveries to Xántus, and his name is included in the scientific designations of dozens of species peculiar to southern Baja. He was among the first to prove how rich Baja is in unique species and biological curiosities.

Sitting on the rocks at Cabo San Lucas, we found it easy to understand why the notion so long persisted that Baja California was an island. There is an island feeling to much of the peninsula, a sense of impregnable remoteness, of being shut off and set apart from the rest of the world—particularly here in the southernmost 125-mile stretch of Baja, the section the white man first knew. At no point in this area is one ever more than 20 miles from the sea, either the Gulf of California or the Pacific Ocean.

But is Baja that isolated, that impregnable? Unfortunately the answer is no. A paved highway now extends from Cabo San Lucas almost halfway up the peninsula and is moving farther north every day. Another highway is coming south from the United States border and will soon plunge into real desert country—and the link-up cannot be far away. The vehicular congestion of Alta California and much of the rest of the United States is already spilling over into Baja. Jet airplanes link La Paz with the rest of Mexico and the United States. Modern car ferries connect La Paz with Mazatlán, Topolobampo and Guaymas on the Mexican mainland. Isolation is disappearing fast. Will it be fatal?

Whenever questions like this bother me, my thoughts return to Guadalupe Island. Guadalupe's history is a sad one, and perhaps significant in terms of what man can do to isolated places. This 100-square-mile island is the loneliest and most isolated part of Baja—almost 150 miles offshore in the Pacific. Under these conditions Guadalupe was once home to many endemic species. Among the trees, for instance, there were Guadalupe fan palms, Guadalupe cypresses, Guadalupe pines.

There were once at least 42 species and subspecies of birds, of which nine were endemic.

But only minimal contact with man virtually destroyed the island as a biological display case. The 19th Century whalers and sealers who came to the island to hunt—and almost exterminate—the Guadalupe fur seals and elephant seals nearly obliterated land life as well, without intending to. To ensure a self-replenishing supply of meat for their crews, they introduced goats and turned them loose on the island, where they proceeded to multiply as goats do. The whalers also introduced cats; the cats went wild and multiplied faster than the goats.

The goats grazed the island bare. They chewed limbs from trees as high as they could reach and, more seriously, devoured seedlings and saplings. A few of the rare native trees survive only in the most inaccessible locations, and there are no young trees on the island. Native ground cover also disappeared under the goats' onslaught, to be replaced, when replaced at all, by weeds.

Destruction of the trees and plant life on Guadalupe robbed the birds of both food and nesting places. The hungry cats did the rest, dispatching most of the birds except the big native caracaras, which are too large, quick and tough for the cats. But the caracaras did not escape either; men tending the goats suspected them of killing young kids and systematically poisoned or shot them.

A ban imposed by the Mexican government in 1922 on the killing of elephant seals and fur seals made it possible for these almost-extinct species to survive and recuperate. But on the island itself the goats and cats continued to multiply—as did the damage they wrought. In recent years many of the goats—their number had been estimated as high as 30,000—have been hunted and killed, the meat and skins processed commercially, but there are still too many. If the goats can be eliminated, the cypress and pine forests will partially regenerate, but many kinds of plants and birds are lost forever. No one has yet suggested what can be done about the cats. Or man.

Guadalupe Island suffered all its calamities while in a state of almost total isolation. The parts of the Baja Peninsula that are similarly isolated are also under threat. Heavy-duty vehicles and light planes can reach sections of Baja previously uncontaminated by man and machines. The lure of the wilderness is drawing more and more visitors, some of them properly appreciative of a rare and strange environment, but too many of them thoughtless and destructive.

The Mexican government has a good record in conservation matters generally and in Baja California particularly. In addition to the decree protecting the seals of Guadalupe Island, it has created a sea bird sanctuary on Raza Island in the gulf. National parks have been created in both the Sierra de Juárez and the Sierra de San Pedro Mártir. Most recently Laguna Ojo de Liebre (Scammon's Lagoon) has been made a refuge for gray whales.

The California Academy of Sciences has been interested in all of these steps and influential in bringing some of them about. Recently its director, George Lindsay, recommended that consideration be given to safeguarding other areas that will suffer as the pressures of population and tourism grow. Many of these are arid, uninhabited or almost uninhabited islands such as San Esteban, home of the blotched chuckwalla and the spiny-tailed iguana; San Pedro Mártir with its population of boobies, pelicans and tropic birds; Santa Catalina and its rattleless rattlesnakes; Espíritu Santo with its population of rare black jack rabbits; and the San Benito Islands on the Pacific coast, with their population of elephant seals and California sea lions. Other areas recommended for preservation are not yet—but may soon be—threatened by the demand for resort development. One is the mountainous peninsula that separates Bahía Concepción from the gulf. Another is the high part of the Sierra de la Laguna in the cape region, a well-wooded country rich in both plant and animal life. And last, Dr. Lindsay suggested that thought be given to the creation of a desert park—or series of parks —in the central part of Baja between El Rosario and Bahía Concepción, the habitat of the strangest of Baja's strange desert vegetation.

Baja California has, for centuries, stubbornly resisted the corrosive effects of man's incessant search for wealth. But now there is growing recognition that man's material gain may not be the ultimate purpose of the universe, that wealth is not confined to that which can be melted into bullion, or killed and taken to the marketplace. Wealth may, instead, exist in secret places, in subtle forms, nonnegotiable in any terms other than those of awe and wonder. With this growing recognition Baja California may be able to go on giving pleasure, insight and understanding to the people of this too-crowded planet.

The Stately Stone of San Lucas

Photographer Jay Maisel knew exactly what he was looking for when, at the end of his long picture-taking trek through Baja, he reached Cabo San Lucas at the southern tip of the peninsula. During a previous visit to the cape, Maisel had been captivated by its wave-sculptured rocks, and he was eager to photograph them for this farewell portfolio.

To do so, he spent three days prowling the high curved spine of granitic rock that separates the Pacific from the Gulf of California. He perched on cliffs to photograph the rock-rimmed shoreline from above, and bounced around in a skiff to take sea-level pictures of formations inaccessible by land.

It was no easy matter to capture subtleties of contour and coloration while balancing precariously on high ledges or rocking in a boat. But what made these acrobatic efforts worthwhile for Maisel was the beauty and diversity of the rock forms. Wherever he looked, he found cruelly angular contours that set off shapes as gently undulating as soft ice cream, or crumbly surfaces that contrasted with textures as smooth as varnished wood. Frozen on film, each of these images evokes some kind of subjective association. To

Maisel, the jagged mass of granitic rock that framed the entrance to a wave-hollowed cavern (right) made its interior appear mysterious, timeless, womblike—indeed the apotheosis of all caves.

Another aspect of the cape landscape that fascinated Maisel was the apparent distortion of scale. The absence of man-made reference points made it difficult to judge true size. The photographer found that if he included waves in a picture the rocks took on recognizable dimension; when he did not, the results were often more intriguing. The four powerfully modeled rock surfaces on page 172, for example, all convey the same sense of monumentality, yet the area shown at upper right is only a few feet square while the others are at least four times greater.

While Maisel relished these ambiguities of scale, he helped clarify the problem with the final panoramic view of the cape that appears on pages 178-179. At far left in the photograph stands an isolated crag —the southernmost Baja outpost —perhaps no more than a city block long. It was in this relatively confined setting that Maisel found and photographed most of the seemingly enormous formations pictured here.

A CAVE CARVED OUT BY OCEAN WAVES

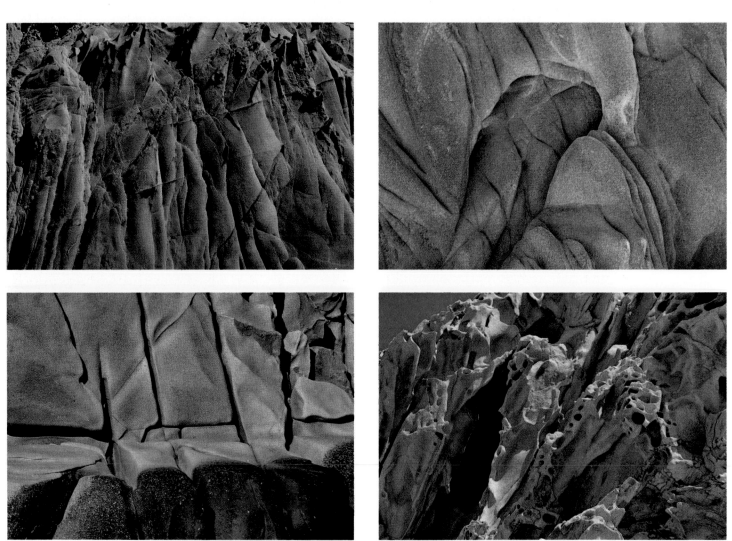

VARIETIES OF NATURAL SCULPTURE

BOULDERS BENEATH A PACIFIC-SIDE CLIFF

SEA BIRDS AND SAND ON A GULF-SIDE BEACH

AN INLET ROUGHHEWN BY HIGH TIDES

A MEETING OF ROCK AND SURF AT THE GULF'S EDGE

CABO SAN LUCAS BATHED BY A SETTING SUN

Bibliography

*Also available in paperback.
†Available in paperback only.

Aschmann, Homer, *The Central Desert of Baja California: Demography and Ecology.* Manessier Publishing Company, 1967.

Britton, N. L., and J. N. Rose, *The Cactaceae.* Dover Publications, 1963.

Cannon, Ray, *The Sea of Cortez.* Lane Magazine & Book Company, 1966.

Clavigero, Francisco Javier, *The History of (Lower) California.* Translated from Italian by Sara E. Lake, Manessier Publishing Company, 1971.

*Dawson, E. Yale, *Cacti of California.* University of California Press, 1966.

Dunne, Peter Masten, *Black Robes in Lower California.* University of California Press, 1968.

†Ellsberg, Helen, *Los Coronados Islands.* La Siesta Press, 1970.

Gardner, Erle Stanley, *The Hidden Heart of Baja.* William Morrow & Company, 1962.

Gerhard, Peter, and Howard E. Gulick, *Lower California Guidebook.* Arthur H. Clark Company, 1970.

Hicks, Sam, *Desert Plants and People.* The Naylor Company, 1966.

Jaeger, Edmund C., *The North American Deserts.* Stanford University Press, 1957.

Kelley, Don Greame, *Edge of a Continent.* American West Publishing Company, 1971.

Klauber, Laurence M., *Rattlesnakes: Their Habits, Life Histories and Influence on Mankind,* 2 vols. University of California Press, 1956.

*Krutch, Joseph Wood, *Baja California and the Geography of Hope.* Sierra Club, 1967.

Krutch, Joseph Wood, *The Forgotten Peninsula.* William Sloane Associates, 1961.

Leopold, A. Starker, *The Desert.* Life Nature Library, TIME-LIFE BOOKS, 1969.

Lewis, Leland R., *Baja Sea Guide.* Miller Freeman Publications, 1971.

McClane, A. J., *McClane's Standard Fishing Encyclopedia.* Holt, Rinehart and Winston, 1965.

MacGinitie, G. E., and Nettie MacGinitie, *Natural History of Marine Animals.* McGraw-Hill, 1968.

Matthews, Leonard Harrison, *The Whale.* Simon and Schuster, 1968.

*Marx, Wesley, *The Frail Ocean.* Coward, 1970.

*Munz, Philip A., and David D. Keck, *California Spring Wildflowers.* University of California Press, 1961.

Nelson, Edward W., *Lower California and Its Natural Resources.* Manessier Publishing Company, 1966.

Nordhoff, Walter, *The Journey of the Flame.* Houghton Mifflin Company, 1955.

Peterson, Roger Tory, *A Field Guide to Western Birds,* 2d ed. Houghton Mifflin Company, 1969.

Pough, Richard H., *Audubon Water Bird Guide.* Doubleday, 1957.

*Raven, Peter H., *Native Shrubs of Southern California.* University of California Press, 1966.

†Scammon, Charles M., *The Marine Mammals of the Northwestern Coast of North America.* Dover Publications, 1968.

Shreve, Forrest, and Ira L. Wiggins, *Vegetation and Flora of the Sonoran Desert.* Stanford University Press, 1964.

*Steinbeck, John, and E. F. Ricketts, *Log from the Sea of Cortez.* Viking Press, 1951.

†*Sunset Travel Guide to Baja California.* Lane Books, 1971.

Sykes, Godfrey, *Colorado Delta.* Kennikat Press, Inc., 1970.

Waters, Frank, *The Colorado.* Rinehart Company, 1946.

Wibberley, Leonard, *Yesterday's Land.* Ives Washburn, Inc., 1961.

Acknowledgments

The author and editors of this book wish to thank the following persons and institutions in California: Gina Alejandre, Chula Vista; Clarence R. Allen, Professor of Geology and Geophysics, California Institute of Technology, Pasadena; Manuel Muñoz Aviña, Los Angeles; Mrs. Griffing Bancroft, La Jolla; Ken Bates, Santa Barbara; Bill Bridges, Los Angeles; William A. Burns, Executive Director, San Diego Natural History Museum; Annetta Carter, Research Associate, Herbarium, Department of Botany, University of California, Berkeley; Robert Cooke, Pasadena; Harry Crosby, La Jolla; Helen DuShane, Whittier; Raymond M. Gilmore, La Jolla; Robert A. Gross, Kentfield; Lallé Hoffman, Los Angeles; Carl L. Hubbs, Professor Emeritus of Biology, Scripps Institution of Oceanography, La Jolla; Joseph Jehl, Curator of Birds and Mammals, San Diego Natural History Museum; Payne Johnson, Del Mar; Lawrence C. Kuebler, Bonita; Enid Larson, Big Pine; Bud Lewis, Los Angeles; William and Betty Mackintosh, Chula Vista; Thomas E. Mahnken Jr., Del Mar; William McIntyre, Laguna; Clement W. Meighan, Professor of Anthropology, University of California, Los Angeles; Larry L. Mayer, Los Angeles; Ralph Miller, San Diego; Thomas Mitchell, Warner Springs; Reid Moran, Curator of Botany, San Diego Natural History Museum; William J. Morris, Professor of Geology, Occidental College, Glendale; Francisco Muñoz, El Cajon; Jay D. Murray, California Institute of Technology, Pasadena; Robert T. Orr, Associate Director, California Academy of Sciences, San Francisco; Betty Hamerly Pappenhagen, Moraga; Richard P. Phillips, La Jolla; Braxton Pollard, Santee; Alexander and Walter B. Power, Redlands; Dale W. Rice, National Marine Fisheries Service, La Jolla; David Roderick, Associate Professor of Chemistry, Foothill College, Palo Alto; Arnold Senterfitt, Lakeside; Allan J. Sloan, Curator of Herpetology, San Diego Natural History Museum; Jack Smith, Los Angeles; Donald E. Walker, Professor of Sociology and Public Administration, San Diego State College; Theodore J. Walker, La Jolla; Ira L. Wiggins, Professor Emeritus of Botany, Stanford University; Librarians and staffs of the libraries at: California Academy of Sciences, San Francisco; San Diego Natural History Museum; San Diego city and county libraries; University of California, Los Angeles; University of California, San Diego. In Baja California: Mr. and Mrs. Richard Adcock, La Paz; Eliseo García Araujo, Mexicali; Aida Meling Barré, San Telmo; Mr. and Mrs. Antero Diaz, Bahía de los Angeles; Gaston and Eric Flourié, Ensenada; Ernesto Raul López, Mexicali; Mr. and Mrs. Salve Meling, San Telmo; Carlos Riva Palacio and Ricardo Garcia Soto, Dirección General de Planeación y Promoción Económico del Territorio de Baja California, La Paz. They also wish to thank the following: Ann Guilfoyle, Senior Editor, *Audubon,* National Audubon Society, New York City; Sidney Horenstein, Department of Invertebrate Paleontology, The American Museum of Natural History, New York City; Ida Novi, Mexico City.

Picture Credits

The sources for the pictures in this book are shown below.

The cover and all photographs by Jay Maisel except pages 8, 9—David Cavagnaro. 18, 19—Map by R. R. Donnelley Cartographic Services. 22—NASA courtesy LIFE. 25—Harry Crosby. 28 —Harry Crosby. 34 through 46—Maps by Margo Dryden. 61 through 71—David Cavagnaro. 92—Robert T. Orr. 120, 121—Jeff Meyer from Animals Animals. 124—Thase Daniel. 126, 127—Thase Daniel. 131 through 137—John Blaustein. 140—Philippe Cousteau. 142, 143 —David Cavagnaro. 144—Theodore J. Walker. 146, 147—Left Flip Schulke from Black Star; right Ron Church. 151 —David Cavagnaro. 155—David Cavagnaro. 156, 157—Left David Cavagnaro; right Alfred L. Pentis. 158 through 161 —David Cavagnaro.

Index

Numerals in italics indicate a photograph or drawing of the subject mentioned.

Printed in U.S.A. **X**